Praise for *Knockout CV*

"You write a CV for a purpose – to get a job. *Knockout CV* works backwards from the desired result, analysing each feature of the CV from the perspective of impact on the decision-maker. No frills, no diversions, simply full of practical help."

Shirley Anderson, HR Director, Talent and Reward, Pilkington Group Limited

"This book is essential reading for anyone considering a career move or applying for another position. First impressions are so important and your CV really does have to stand out from all the rest. This is an excellent, practical guide which I believe will really make the difference to securing that interview."

Christine Gaskell, Chair, Cheshire and Warrington Local Enterprise Partnership & former HR Director, Bentley Motors Ltd

"John Lees leads you back to the basic document of so many job-hunting campaigns, and yet again opens your eyes to see the real underlying principles. His clear and authoritative voice brings life back into what is often seen as a routine activity – CV writing – yet is so important in today's hyper-competitive job market. With his clear chapter objectives, insightful exercises (especially the 'CV data bank'), professional insights, and a healthy dose of humour, John Lees sets the standard for modern CV writing."

Matthias Feist, Head of Careers & Business Relations at Regent's University London, UK and Chair of PlaceNet: Placements in Industry Network

"John has produced an honest and authentic approach to creating a winning CV which speaks to your strengths, and will make the difference to getting noticed and in front of the selection panel. Yes, you can expect to work some, however John's advice plus your investment in time will produce a great result with the critical bonus of mental and emotional clarity over your next (right) career move."

Angella Clarke-Jervoise, Big 4 Partner Recruiter and International Career Coach

Praise for John Lees' careers books

"When I read John's writing, two things happen. First, I feel as if he's standing right there, personally advising me. And second, I always come away thinking over the issue in a new way. It's a rare, but very useful, gift."

Sarah Green, Associate Editor, *Harvard Business Review*

"I know first-hand the joy that being in the right career can bring and I commend John Lees for his books and seminars which help other people do just that."

Rosemary Conley CBE

"John Lees is the Career Professional's professional; the doyen of careers experts. His books and advice have helped countless numbers of people to enjoy better, more fulfilling careers."

Dr Harry Freedman, Career and Business Strategist, Hanover Executive

"John Lees' approach works, because he gives readers simple, practical steps to help flip their mindsets into the more daring, exploratory and confident mode needed for career transition success."

Stuart Lindenfield, Head of Transitions Practice, Reed Consulting

"*How to Get a Job You'll Love* is a treasure. Read it, devour it, use it, and find that job you once dreamed about but had almost given up on."

Richard Nelson Bolles, author of *What Color Is Your Parachute?*

"I frequently recommend job seekers or those at a career crossroads to read *How to Get a Job You'll Love* as it offers practical and easily accessible advice from someone with vast experience in the area."

Joëlle Warren, Managing Director, Warren Partners Ltd

"Highly recommended – always practical, but never patronising."

Ian Wylie, former Editor, *Guardian Work*

"John Lees' books provide practical, jargon-free advice for jobseekers. He keeps readers focused on achieving what they really want from their career – rather than worrying about what they don't want."

Karen Dempsey, former Editor, *Personnel Today*

"The popularity of John Lees' writing lies in his ability to connect with the sense many people have that they can be more than they currently are and deserve greater job satisfaction than they currently have. What makes his work distinctive is his use of his wide experience in careers coaching to provide tools and ways of thinking that any motivated individual can easily use to take control of their working life."

Carole Pemberton, Career and Executive Coach and author of *Coaching To Solutions*

Knockout CV

How to get noticed, get interviewed *and* get hired

John Lees

The **McGraw·Hill** *Companies*

London • Boston • Burr Ridge, IL • Dubuque, IA • Madison WI • New York
San Francisco • St. Louis • Bangkok • Bogotá • Caracas • Kuala Lumpur
Lisbon • Madrid • Mexico City • Milan • Montreal • New Delhi • Santiago
Seoul • Singapore • Sydney • Taipei • Toronto

Knockout CV: How to get noticed, get interviewed and get hired

John Lees

ISBN-13: 9780077152857
ISBN-10: 0077152859
e-ISBN: 9780077152864

 **Professional**

Published by:
McGraw-Hill Education
Shoppenhangers Road, Maidenhead, Berkshire, England SL6 2QL
Telephone: 44 (0) 1628 502500
Fax: 44 (0) 1628 770224
Website: www.mcgraw-hill.co.uk

British Library Cataloguing in Publication Data
A catalogue record for this book is available from the British Library

McGraw-Hill books are great for training, as gifts, and for promotions.
Please contact our corporate sales executive to discuss special quantity
discounts or customisation to support your initiatives: b2b@mcgraw-hill.com.

Typeset and designed by Gray Publishing, Tunbridge Wells
Printed and bound by CPI Group (UK) Ltd, Croydon, CR0 4YY

Contents

Foreword

With 20 years in career management behind us at Fairplace and CMC we understand the value of a good CV and how as a 'shop window' it has become more critical in these increasingly digital and competitive times. We know that most CVs get a brief scan at best, so they need to stand out while remaining professional and accessible. One spelling mistake or an odd or challenging format will turn the reader off and they will move on to the next CV. The quality of the communication required to create a compelling CV in two pages is the focus of this book.

We have found that distilling skills, experience and attributes and conveying them well is not something many candidates are accustomed to doing. This book can help as a pragmatic and accessible distillation of what looks good in a CV and importantly why it looks good. It will help you understand the CV's purpose and its market, so that you can hit the bull's eye. Rather than take a cookie-cutter approach, the book's advice helps you to reveal the best version of yourself, challenging the writer to craft a distinctive CV using real examples and illustrations to bring the points to life. This is important to ensure that your CV, although a self-marketing tool, remains authentic and fresh and is a true reflection of you.

In todays' digital world the CV has a rapidly evolving purpose. With social networking and social media increasingly important in job searching, the traditional CV is no longer appropriate; CV writers need to be aware of this and use it to their advantage. Having helped thousands of people find new roles, we understand that getting your CV to work for you on every level remains a major competitive advantage. Sadly, it is often not what people see as a priority, simply listing what they have done, overusing tired phrases and confusing the reader with jargon and clumsy formats. The signal value alone that a CV sends out about an individual and their abilities is significant. This book is timely in that the shifting employment and digital landscapes require a different approach. Understanding the pitfalls as well as the opportunities in this new environment is critical.

We were pleased to have our clients participate in informing this book to help give it both reality and currency. One of the many insights gleaned from this market view is the need to create a CV that matches your career stage. And instead of railing against pigeon-holing, this can be reshaped as an advantage when you know what the person reading your CV is looking for. From CV draft to final edit, the book's direct and disciplined style delivers a real punch and will be a useful tool for anyone serious about their job search.

Penny de Valk, CEO of Fairplace Cedar

About the author

John Lees is one of the UK's best-known career strategists. *How To Get A Job You'll Love* regularly tops the list as the bestselling careers book by a British author, and along with *Job Interviews: Top Answers To Tough Questions* has been selected as WH Smith's 'Business Book of the Month'.

As a career and outplacement coach, John specialises in helping people make difficult career decisions – difficult either because they don't know what to do next or because there are barriers in the way of success. John Lees Associates helps career changers across the UK. John is a regular keynote speaker, has presented at the world's largest international career conferences, and has run workshops in the USA, Switzerland, South Africa, Australia, and New Zealand.

John is the author of a wide range of career titles. He has been a regular columnist for *Metro* and *People Management* and has written thought leadership pieces for *The Guardian* and *The Times*. He is featured in the national press and his work has been profiled in *Management Today*, *Psychologies*, *Coaching at Work*, and the *Sunday Times*. John broadcasts widely and has contributed to BBC Two's 'Working Lunch', Channel 4's 'Dispatches', ITV's 'Tonight – How To Get A Job', and BBC Radio 4's 'Woman's Hour'. He is a regular blog contributor to *Harvard Business Review* online and in 2012 wrote the introduction to the *HBR Guide to Getting the Right Job*.

John is a graduate of the universities of Cambridge, London, and Liverpool, and has spent most of his career focusing on the world of work. He has trained recruitment specialists since the mid-1980s, and is the former Chief Executive of the Institute of Employment Consultants. He has worked with a large range of organisations including British Gas Commercial, The British Council, Career Management Consultants Ltd, CIPD, Cranfield School of Management, Hiscox, The House of Commons, Imperial College, Orange, REC, The Association of MBAs, Lloyds Banking Group, Marks & Spencer, and Reuters, as well as business schools across the UK. John is a Fellow of the CIPD, an Honorary Fellow of the Institute of Recruitment Professionals, and a Career Management Fellow. Until 2013 he served as Joint Chair of ACPi-UK and was a founding board member of the Career Development Institute.

Alongside his careers work John serves as an ordained Anglican priest in the Diocese of Chester. He lives and works in Cheshire, with his wife, children's writer and poet, Jan Dean, with occasional visits from their two adult sons.

John Lees Associates provides one-to-one career coaching in most parts of the UK. For details plus information about talks and workshops given by John Lees visit www.johnleescareers.com.

Readers of John's books are welcome to join the LinkedIn networking and discussion group 'How To Get A Job You'll Love Network' – search for it in groups within LinkedIn.

Other careers books by John Lees published by McGraw-Hill Professional

How To Get A Job You'll Love (2012), £14.99, ISBN 0077140222

John Lees' definitive career book, now in its seventh edition. A single-volume career-coaching programme designed to help everyone who has found themselves saying 'I want to do something different, but I don't know what it is'. *'This book is a treasure. Read it, devour it, use it, and find that job you once dreamed about but had almost given up on.'* Richard Nelson Bolles, author of *What Color Is Your Parachute?*

Job Interviews: Top Answers To Tough Questions (2012), £9.99, ISBN 0077141601

An insider's view of the job interview, this third edition lists tried and tested strategies for overcoming nerves and being the best version of you on the day. Details 225 interview questions typically asked by employers and recruiters including off-the-wall and probing questions that will throw you completely unless you prepare carefully.

Take Control of Your Career (2006), £12.99, ISBN 0077109677

How to manage your career once you've got a job, learning how to read your organisation, avoid career traps, renegotiate your job role and enhance your future without losing control of your life balance.

Career Reboot – 24 Tips for Tough Times (2009), £9.99, ISBN 0077127589

Packed with quick-read, practical tips for rejuvenating your job search, this book is a must for anyone striking out into a difficult job market after redundancy or simply looking for new opportunities in a difficult market.

Acknowledgements

After over a decade of producing books I am getting better at thanking people properly. I owe a huge debt to Richard Nelson Bolles, author of the world-famous *What Color Is Your Parachute?* My work as a career strategist was inspired by the creativity, wisdom, and generosity of 125 hours' teaching from Dick Bolles at two of his summer workshops in Bend, Oregon, and over a decade of encouragement and support.

Two people have made an enormous difference to this book. First, thanks to Gill Best for everything she does as friend, coach, and colleague – and very particularly for her detailed comments on the first draft. A huge thank-you also to Kate Howlett, Managing Consultant at John Lees Associates, for taking the book in a whole new direction with her exciting new thinking about the way CVs are read.

My heartfelt thanks go to Career Management Consultants Ltd, part of the Savile Group, for commissioning the CV survey outlined in this book. Thanks also to Keith Busfield, Linda Clark, Graeme Dixon, Zena Everett, Jeff Grout, Stuart McIntosh, Joëlle Warren, and Ruth Winden for their incisive contributions.

I would like to extend my thanks to my editor Monika Lee and to the whole McGraw-Hill team, particularly James Heath, and to my agent James Wills at Watson, Little for his unstinting support. My appreciation goes to Becky Charman for her first-class PR management. Finally, I remember with sadness and huge appreciation my talented publicist and dear friend Sue Blake (1961–2012): it wouldn't have been half as much fun without you.

This book is dedicated to my sons, Matthew and Christopher, the greatest of chaps, both out there hacking a path through the work jungle.

Overview: composing your CV from back to front

Think about what you want your CV to do for you and how you will use it in your job search

(Chapters 1–2)

⬇

Understand the way your CV will be interpreted, and why CVs fail to gain attention

(Chapter 3 and Appendix)

⬇

Catalogue the raw material of your experience into a CV data bank

(Chapter 4)

⬇

Decide on a format and structure which suits your needs

(Chapters 5–7)

⬇

Learn how to turn past events into well-written CV evidence

(Chapter 8)

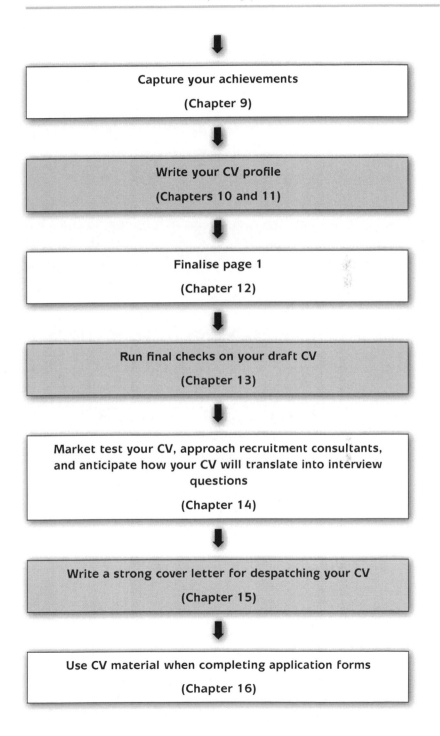

List of downloadable documents and CVs

If you would like larger, A4 versions of these documents they can be downloaded free from www.johnleescareers.com/downloads.asp. All you need to do is register on the website, which is also free of charge.

Download	Page
Documents and worksheets	
Skill sampling grid (Chapter 4)	44
Skills and challenges checklist (Chapter 8)	91
Cover letter (Chapter 15)	163
Example CVs included in the book	
CV with a profile: Deirdre Prospect CV (Chapter 3)	30
Second job: James Steady CV (Chapter 7)	73
Simple page 1: Alison Nameless CV page 1 (Chapter 7)	70
Events manager: Sara Workhard CV (Chapter 12)	133
Example CVs not included in the book	
Straight-in CV	
School leaver CV	
College leaver CV	
Graduate CV	
Executive CV with profile	
Executive CV with extended profile	

Using the JLA Skill Cards to help you produce a knockout CV

The New JLA Skill Card sort offers a step-by-step guide to identifying your motivated skills. Full instructions are provided to enable you to gather evidence of achievement, rehearse focused mini-narratives, and use that evidence in writing a CV or preparing for a job interview.

Simply quote reference SKL 2013 to purchase a card sort at a discounted price of £18.00 including postage (normal price £22.75) – UK and Republic of Ireland only.

Email info@johnleescareers.com to take advantage of this special offer.

Why you should read this book

Three trays

Imagine a busy manager reading your CV. In a healthy market this decision-maker might have three trays in which to place your CV: *yes*, *no*, and *maybe*. In a tough market, there is no *maybe* pile. Your CV has got to work, immediately. Most don't.

Seeking a quick fix for your CV problems? This strategy will probably extend your job search. You won't know what's working, or what to change. You will waste the time of employers by making them read early drafts that you haven't market tested.

It doesn't take months to learn how to write a CV that works, but it does take a few hours. This book is designed to take you through that process quickly, taking some short cuts, encouraging your readers to say one simple word: 'yes'.

If your aim is to find a job fast, start thinking differently. Many of our clients arrive saying 'I'm trying to get my head around my CV'. I admire that. It shows that they understand that a good CV is a reflection of a thought process, not simply a catalogue of facts. It's a smart, effective summary of who you are and what you can offer. Learn to see the world through the eyes of the people who make hiring decisions, and understand how to communicate your best qualities quickly, attractively, and in a convincing voice.

The Internet is full of free careers advice and downloadable CV examples. So why should you read another CV book?

The problem is that CV writing looks simple. Surely it's just a matter of dropping the right information in the right places? In reality the process isn't just about writing a document – it's about shaping the way people think about you. It's about adopting job search strategies where people pass on details of your strengths until finally you persuade someone to employ you. It's about asking people you don't know very well to take you seriously. This subtle process of planting ideas, persuasion, and breaking through isn't anywhere near as simple as it looks.

For readers familiar with my earlier work *Why You? – CV Messages To Win Jobs* I can confirm that the models used in this new book are quite different in terms of layout and thinking. The market has moved on considerably since that book was published in 2007.

There are some very good CV books out there. Here's a few reasons why this book might solve your problems in ways that others won't:

- It reflects decades of experience in recruitment and career management; working closely with employers, HR specialists, recruitment consultants, and thousands of job hunters.
- It builds on tried and tested strategies for predicting the way your CV will be read.
- Its recommendations draw on real results of CVs that get people shortlisted. Theory is exciting; results count.
- This book is based on hard evidence: research conducted among employers and external recruiters on the things that get you shortlisted, and the things that get you left out.
- It draws not just on my opinion but the expertise of many others in this field, trusted colleagues. Sometimes they have views different to my own, and where they do, I will tell you.

■ It contains strategies and approaches you won't find anywhere else.

■ It connects with the rest of my work, particularly *How To Get A Job You'll Love* and *Job Interviews: Top Answers To Tough Questions*.

I don't just want you to get a job, I want you to get a job that feels right at least three days out of five. I want your CV to communicate the very best version of you.

Making your
CV work for you

This chapter helps you to:

- Understand the power and impact of a well-pitched CV
- Understand how your document will be read
- Avoid over-reliance on your CV in job searching
- Begin to see your CV as part of a broader, coherent message

> *'You don't write because you want to say something, you write because you have something to say.'*   F. Scott Fitzgerald

Your life on paper

You know what can go wrong when your CV hits the desk of a decision-maker. It may be misinterpreted. Important details may be overlooked. Your strongest points may be missed, but the reader may pay close attention to things you didn't want to emphasise. You rely heavily on your CV to persuade people to shortlist you, but if you're trying to make a career change your CV may work against you.

If you have spent hours crafting a CV it may come as a disappointment to realise that few people out there look forward to reading it. Reading CVs is a relatively dull, uninspiring task, often put off until late in the evening when a tired mind struggles to find anything relevant, let alone interesting.

There are many urban myths in circulation about how quickly CVs are read. It's unlikely to be more than five minutes even in the most painstaking of organisations. Even full-time recruitment specialists admit that the first run at a CV takes about 15–20 seconds. HR professionals are often responsible for recruitment, so may have other things they would rather be doing. For the busy line manager, reading CVs is a distraction from getting results. People who see dozens of CVs every day learn how to fillet them very quickly for important information. Readers make snap judgements, and look for obvious indicators that you fit the job and it makes sense as your next step.

There's no point doing much work on your CV until you understand:

- CV features most likely to get you into the interview room.
- CV features most likely to put employers off.

Throughout this book you'll be reminded of these two issues in depth. You can also see the results of an employer survey of what employers love and hate in the Appendix: **Employer responses to the CV survey** on pages 177–84.

In the past, only the professional classes needed a CV. Today, most people need a CV at some stage in their lives, either when job hunting or when applying for a course or a grant. CVs are read on paper, online, on smart phones (it may be read by computer software, although this happens less often than you might think). The document you spend hours drafting will sometimes be glanced at rather than read, perhaps by someone with only a passing understanding of the role in question. Even in this age of social media a CV is a vital tool that can get you in front of some very interesting people.

So why don't we spend more time and thought when writing CVs? Too many people are happy to download poor templates from the Internet and adapt them with little attention. As we will see from the research outlined in this book, the documents produced are often unhelpful, unbalanced, and unproductive.

Are you relying on your CV too much?

How much will you rely on your CV? Some people chart their way through a successful career without ever attending an interview, and never need a CV. Others change jobs regularly yet hardly ever use a CV – jobs are found, and offered, informally.

Many people lean heavily on their CV to do a wide range of things: get them noticed, shortlisted, get a job offer. The problem is that a CV isn't always the best tool. For example, even the most half-hearted networking will always open more doors to new organisations than your CV. If a CV is required by an employer, send it. However, too many people believe the best way of establishing or confirming a relationship is to send over a CV. Often, as this book outlines, asking someone to read your CV kills the conversation stone dead.

What a CV *really* does for you

Too often CV writing is seen as the one critical step between you and getting a job. It isn't. A CV opens up the possibility of a conversation. In a tight market, getting on to a shortlist requires an above-average document. That's a lot to ask from a few sheets of paper, so, word for word, line for line, your CV is probably going to work a lot harder than most things you've written.

When you start job hunting it's vital to do some thinking; reflect on your situation and how you got here. If you've been made redundant or you have been out of the market for some time, think carefully about how you're going to deal with that. Proper reflection also means looking at yourself. Look at things you find it difficult to get across – gaps in your work history, changes of direction, a course you dropped out of … You'll almost certainly need to spend time dredging up good evidence from your past, and polishing it so it gets you results. Thinking also means planning: preparing carefully for a well-conducted job hunt efficient enough to get you a job offer before you run out of energy or money.

As a career coach I get a great many phone calls and emails from people who say 'please sort my CV out for me'. Most of them have missed out two vital steps. First, they don't really know what they want to say about themselves, and second they have little idea where their CV is going. How would you feel if you were asked to sell a product you don't really understand to customers you know nothing about?

The perfect CV

Many jobseekers have a CV that fails to get them shortlisted – not because of a lack of skills or experience, simply because it under-functions. They believe, quite wrongly, that with a perfect CV, job searching would be a breeze. You don't need a perfect CV, you need the best document you are capable of writing. The best candidate doesn't always get shortlisted for interview – those with the most effective CVs do.

A CV isn't there to get you a job. It's there to get you into a meeting. This might be an interview (with an employer or with a recruitment consultant), it might be a networking meeting, it might be the opportunity to pitch for a piece of work. In other words, a CV is a piece of communication that has only one purpose: to get you into a room with someone who can influence your future.

What overall message does your CV convey?

There are, potentially, hundreds of things you could tell an employer. Some of these facts would be relevant, interesting, and memorable, most won't be. Your CV needs to be detailed, but not comprehensive. It doesn't need to say everything. The art of getting noticed is about *planting just enough information in the minds of decision-makers.*

Anyone who meets you, reads your CV, or looks you up on LinkedIn needs to understand your message.

Your message

- The minimum information required to get maximum attention.
- The right information at the right time to the right people.
- The most memorable content from your CV, covering letters, LinkedIn page, and what you say in person about yourself.
- Short, focused, communication bursts which result in buying signals from decision-makers.

The 'decision-makers' referred to here include high-level networking contacts and recruitment agencies as well as prospective employers. Buying signals include a range of behaviours such as phone calls, speculative calls from recruitment consultants, an invitation to attend an interview, and ultimately a job offer.

Your CV is one communication channel among many. In a good job search you'll use several channels simultaneously:

- **paper** – in CVs, application forms and cover letters
- **email** – cover messages attaching your CV, in requests for information or contacts, in follow-ups after meetings
- **phone** conversations with existing and new contacts

■ **face-to-face meetings** with everyone from friends, work colleagues, good contacts, and every kind of decision-maker ranging from recruitment consultants to industry experts to hiring employers.

All of these messages combine and have a tangible result: what people remember about you, and *what they say about you if your name comes up in conversation*. With people just as much as products, we remember features we find attractive. So your overall combination of messages needs to be:

■ simple
■ memorable
■ easily communicated
■ coherent.

Simplicity is the key to good design. A **simple** CV gets the right messages across quickly, in uncomplicated, direct language that doesn't get in the way. The format should be helpful with the vital information being easy to find. A CV which is **memorable** means that important facts get passed on when you are not present. Your name comes up in conversation when you're not in the room. If your best points are **easily communicated** you won't sound like a hopeful outsider but like someone already doing the job – using language which matches the mindset of the employer. Being **coherent** means telling one straightforward, consistent story.

Weak CVs contain contradictory messages and offer several conflicting storylines. The result is that a reader becomes confused ('I can't work out whether you're a frustrated entrepreneur or just someone who hasn't had the right big company experience yet' or 'Your CV sends me in several directions simultaneously – I can't work out where to place you'). Being coherent encourages **healthy pigeon-holing** (see Chapter 12, pages 128–9). Yes, you're put in a pigeon-hole, but it's one which actively assists your job search. Help people to understand what kinds of jobs you are looking for. Avoid phrasing like 'looking for a general management position' – if you leave the CV reader struggling to name your next job, you probably won't get it.

Being coherent also means that the style, content, and 'feel' of your covering letter and CV should match your interview performance. Recruiters commonly complain that a very different person walks in the door to the one they were expecting. Communicate the real you, not your cartoon picture of an identikit candidate.

Employer cynicism about CVs

Few recruiters out there will believe everything you put on paper. Occupational psychologists have for many years written about 'impression management' – the way candidates attempt to manipulate the perception of the recruiter. Some HR specialists use the phrase as if it means lying. It doesn't – many occasions at work when you're trying to influence someone involve impression management: in a sales meeting you want to appear knowledgeable and trustworthy, in a negotiation you want to appear confident, in a meeting with your boss you may want to appear focused, creative, or decisive.

It's perfectly acceptable to think about the way your overall message works – and how it shapes the way people see you. The important thing is to reveal *the best version of yourself.* Do bear in mind, however, that selectors are highly tuned to information that seems overblown, improbable, or just plain false. Be aware that your CV will be read by someone busy, unsympathetic to your long-term career needs. Your reader will also be easily irritated by CV layout and style that gets in the way (see Chapter 5).

Your reader may also start with the assumption that you're not telling the truth. Our research (see the Appendix, pages 177–84) confirms that decision-makers are hesitant about believing CV claims. The other side of the coin is that if you're writing a CV you are under considerable pressure to provide accurate and reliable information. As one employer put it *'better the reliable, dull candidate than the exciting dud'*.

Key points from this chapter

✓ In a tough market your CV has to work effectively and quickly to get into the *yes* tray.
✓ Your CV doesn't get you the job, it just gets you a meeting.
✓ You don't need a perfect CV, but one that gets you in the door and reflects the best version of you.
✓ Every part of the job search process is about impression management and managing the things you communicate.
✓ Begin to think about your CV as a short collection of key messages that you want influential people to remember and talk about.

2

Your CV and your job search

This chapter helps you to:

- Use your CV in an effective multi-strategy approach
- Know when to use your CV, and when to keep it under wraps
- Add other key strategies to your job hunting
- Interrogate job advertisements and anticipate the interview questions your CV will trigger

> *'Half the world is composed of people who have something to say and can't, and the other half who have nothing to say and keep on saying it.'* Robert Frost

Job searching on several levels at once

Think about how you're going to use your new CV. If you just chase advertised jobs you may be up against 500-plus applicants – with those odds, even the best CV in the world may not work. Rejection leads to loss of confidence, and it's easy to start trashing your goals. Smart career changers adopt a multi-strategy approach to shorten the odds and cut down your job search time. Careers specialist Keith Busfield, Director of Anderson Yorke Associates, writes: 'Without a clear career strategy, a carefully crafted CV is still only words.'

Research before you job search

The Royal Bank of Scotland Career Start Report researched the amount of time graduates spent on career planning, suggesting that nearly a third of final-year students spent less than a day researching their future. Even less time was spent researching specific employers. Nearly half of the students polled, all applying for graduate schemes, admitted they spent less than a couple of hours researching an organisation before applying. A new permanent job can have a major impact on your career story; quality research is vital.

Do your homework on sectors and likely employers so that you build up a list of potential CV targets. New kinds of jobs are being created all the time, and most of them didn't exist 20 years ago. Finding out about work sectors ultimately also means talking to real people about the jobs they do. This is the first step to successful networking. Exploration is the key – finding out what's out there. The spin-off is that you become visible in the hidden (unadvertised) job market. By asking smart questions, you become perceived as a credible candidate. You may find yourself in a shortlist of one.

Matching your CV to your job search strategy

Here are nine ways you might get good value out of your CV.

1 Exploration

You use your CV to help you discover what roles might be suitable for you. It's quite common for people to use the process of sending out different kinds of CV as a way of testing the market, or as a sounding board to discover where they might fit. Feedback may show you where you need to adapt material or language, and you may be surprised at how transferable your skills are. You'll quickly discover the need to build in face-to-face exploratory discussions.

Disadvantages include the fact that you'll get little feedback on your CV. Also, sending out widely varying versions of your CV can blur your reputation.

2 Optimistic career change strategy

You may hope that your CV will appeal to a wide range of sectors. Sometimes a well-designed CV can open doors; an enlightened reader might make useful connections between your offer and the needs of employers in sectors you haven't yet considered. The downside is that your CV may suggest a lack of focus.

Keith Busfield sets the parameters for this kind of strategy: 'Research or write out your ideal job. Put together the recruitment brief for that role – the key functional responsibilities, required skill sets, experience. Now write the CV matching your experience to the brief. If it doesn't match 90%, then sadly that is a dream job, not a true short–medium term career aspiration.'

3 Sector focus

Writing a CV that aims at one defined sector but fits a broad range of roles is often a successful strategy. Ensure that you convey the right facts in the right language. The CV may need adjustments in language and by providing clues about the job titles you might fill.

4 Role focus

If you are confident that the work you do is pretty much the same across several sectors you can focus your CV on one particular role – but only if you make sure the language you use works in all of your target sectors. Explain enough to demonstrate that your skills are transferable – don't assume that they are.

5 Job specific

At times you will want to match your CV against one particular job. If your CV is well designed you may only need to redraft the profile or primary bullet points on page 1. It may be easier to list your top five or six matching pieces of evidence in a covering letter.

6 Speculative

Part of your strategy may be sending your CV to organisations not currently hiring. Your CV, especially if tailored, might showcase skills and experience immediately required. However, an unrequested CV is often not read with sympathy – if at all – but you may overcome this by writing a strong speculative cover letter (see Chapter 15, pages 164–8) which clearly compares what the organisation needs with what you have to offer.

7 Tight market

Your CV is going to have to work brilliantly where hundreds of people are applying. Naturally, an above-average CV stands a better chance of getting you shortlisted. Often this will be because of an interesting mix of skills and experience rather than because you are unique. Your CV may be lost in a very large crowd, which is why it pays to try to establish relationships with an employer in person or by phone as well as sending in a CV.

8 Relationships and networking

A CV on its own cannot create and sustain networks, but it might be a suitable *aide-mémoire* after someone has met you. Your CV should reinforce the same strong messages you are getting across in networking discussions. Reading a CV and passing it on is a substantial request, so sending the document after a meeting may in fact close down a growing relationship (see 'Reading your CV – the big ask' below on page 17).

9 Online

Managing your online reputation is vital in your job search. Career coach Ruth Winden writes: 'Your CV will neither be the first nor the only impression you will make on a recruiter. What do recruiters see when they search for you online, before they decide to contact you and ask for your CV – be it on LinkedIn, Twitter, Google+ or any of the other social media platforms? And what do they see when they go online, after they have read your CV? Inconsistencies raise doubts and undermine the good impression you are trying to make. Don't confuse recruiters. A confused recruiter won't connect with you, let alone recruit you.'

LinkedIn is the social media channel of choice for jobseekers, employers, and recruitment agencies. Unlike other channels which blur into chat and entertainment, LinkedIn is all about work, so is a sensible place to set out your stall as a candidate. Your LinkedIn page should highlight the same few, vital messages showcased in your CV. Use LinkedIn headlines to capture your main work focus (see **Healthy pigeon-holing** in Chapter 12, page 128). Cover your top skills, experience, and other strengths in the profile. Don't state 'seeking a position' or anything indicating that you're unemployed – your main message is what you have to offer, not what you're trying to get past. Include your LinkedIn URL at the top of your CV.

Recruiter Graeme Dixon, Director of the Oportunis Group, reminds you: 'Look at the email address you use to send the CV. I have seen everything, including sexy101xxx@ and bigmonster@. And if you are sending it via email do you need a postal address?'

Sometimes, possibly less than you think, your CV will be read by a computer. Ruth Winden writes: 'Applicant Tracking Systems (ATS) are programmed to search your CV for key words vital to the role. How can you get over this hurdle? Include the most likely search terms in your CV. Check the job advertisement and job description carefully, research current terminology used in your industry for equivalent roles by scouring advertisements on sites such as www.indeed.co.uk and checking trade magazines. List both common abbreviations and the full-length keyword to beat the ATS software (for example, PM and Project Management; SCM and Supply Chain Management). But don't overstuff your CV with keywords, and only include terms that are a true reflection of your capabilities.'

You can also use white text in your CV for search engine optimisation. JLA's Managing Consultant Kate Howlett advises: 'Use invisible search-engine friendly phrases. In the (otherwise empty) footer type in words and phrases you know will be picked up by search engines. Use a tiny font size and white text so the words are invisible on screen.'

Five Steps to a multi-strategy job search

1 Build up a strong relationship with at least six and up to 20 **recruitment consultancies** (see Chapter 14, page 152). Make sure they understand what you're really looking for by communicating a clear message as often as possible.

2 Learn how to **interrogate job advertisements** (see below), matching your strengths to an employer's short-list in a brief, highly focused covering letter. Sometimes you will also need to complete application forms (see Chapter 16, page 170).

3 Use the **Internet**, particularly the better job boards and organisations' own sites, but don't waste time on the Internet during working hours when you can be following steps 4 and 5.

4 Improve your luck by **talking to people** about what's out there. Keep asking the question 'who else should I be talking to?'. Enthusiasm and a hunger to find new outlets for your talents get you noticed in the hidden (unadvertised) job market.

5 Target organisations directly with a well-pitched letter and CV. These **speculative approaches** to organisations can be surprisingly effective – if you have a good covering letter and a strong CV (see Chapter 15).

Whatever you do, don't skip step 4: warm conversations lead to the greatest breakthroughs. Research sectors by asking around, not through web pages.

Put your CV away and talk to people

It's easy to think that a strong CV is all you need to get a brilliant job. It will increase your chances of being shortlisted, but in itself it's not a strong tool for influencing people. Expecting all this from a CV fails to grasp how people are noticed, recommended, and hired. **If you are relying exclusively on your CV to open doors, you will extend your job search.**

At the beginning of a job search, don't carpet bomb contacts with your CV. It's probably too unfocused and will give you indifferent results. Equally, resist the temptation to send it to every high-level decision-maker in your contact book such as previous bosses, for example. Contact these important people later in the process when your message is clear and you know what two or three things you want from them.

At the beginning of a job search, approach people who you find easy to talk to – family, friends, and work colleagues who you trust. Good first-level contacts should be:

- easy to approach
- positive about your skills and experience (the kind of people who will remind you what you're good at)
- lateral thinkers who will suggest further exploration, and lead you towards the right people and organisations.

Look again at those three criteria: nowhere does it say 'good at editing CVs'. Some of those people might be able to advise you on CV style, others will give you vague or contradictory information. The people you approach at first are good at interpreting *you*, and good at interpreting what's out there. So, don't get locked into your CV at this stage. Just keep a notebook for ideas, and a good record every time somebody reminds you of something for your **CV data bank** (see Chapter 4, pages 37–9, on cataloguing your material).

Follow your curiosity

Now we'll consider the kind of conversations you might have with people you know less well. These are not job interviews, but information-based conversations which help you learn more about target sectors (see the REVEAL method in *How To Get A Job You'll Love*).

Reading your CV – the big ask

Imagine you've had coffee with Jill, HR manager in a large manufacturing firm. She has given you some tremendous insights into your target work sectors. You now know a lot more about industry trends, who is hiring, and about the language employers use to describe top performers. Jill can recommend you to a few contacts, and will probably remember you if a vacancy comes up. Asking Jill to connect on LinkedIn after a warm face-to-face meeting is not a big ask – it's pretty much a done deal.

What's the next step with Jill? After a meeting people are tempted to attach their CV to a 'thank-you' email. Why? *Just in case.* The idea seems to make sense – it could be a memory jogger (but if someone wants to check your experience they can look you up on LinkedIn). You might be seeking feedback on style and content, but that's asking a lot – proper feedback is very time consuming. Your secret hope of course is that your CV will be forwarded to someone who has a vacancy to fill – a referral, such as passing it on to HR. That's an even bigger ask – do you really expect people to put their reputation on the line like that?

Think again. Jill is a busy person. She'll happily read a thank-you note after your meeting. However, if your email includes a CV, the attachment will probably be unopened. *Inviting someone to look at your CV is a big ask.* No one reads a CV unless they have to – it's a chore and may lead to obligations that can't be fulfilled. Whenever you catch yourself saying 'I'll just attach my CV' understand what that action really means:

END OF CONVERSATION.

Your email goes into that folder we secretly label 'I'll get round to it sometime', which means, of course, never. You'll say your networking is going nowhere, but in fact you've turned your CV into a conversation stopper. It does not further the conversation or trigger action.

There *is* one thing you can do after a discussion. This is not about asking for names of contacts – ask for them in the meeting itself (say at the outset that you want to pick some-one's brain and find out who's good to talk to). Yes, do write a note of thanks. Say how and why your contact's advice was helpful and where it led you. And then, rather than attaching your CV, add up to half a dozen short bullet points summa-rising your game plan, for example:

> Hi Jill
>
> Thanks for meeting me yesterday. You gave me some great ideas and, thanks to your introduction to Simon, I know a lot more about interim work.
>
> I really enjoyed our meeting, and I wonder if it would be helpful if I remind you what I am looking for:
>
> - I am looking for a role which builds on my estate and property management experience.
> - I am exploring a range of sectors to find out which roles match my technical and project management skills.
> - Right now I am interested in meeting professionals working in facilities management.

These bullet points are short enough to be read at a glance, and will either stick in the memory or prompt an immediate response. We like emails that we can read quickly and then action. So it's likely that someone will email or telephone someone on your behalf, there and then. If it doesn't happen within 30 seconds of your email arriving, it may never happen at all. You might also use this opportunity to ask one addi-tional question you didn't cover in the meeting – but only if it can be answered easily.

Why you might never use your CV

Imagine for a moment that sending out CVs was against the law. What would you do? The answer isn't difficult. You'd talk to people. In fact, a great many people find jobs without ever writing a CV. This includes school leavers as well as very senior and marketable candidates. They fall across jobs through conversations, connections, sometimes through simple curiosity. A job is offered informally, sometimes created around the candidate.

It's also fair to say that the vast majority of candidates will need a CV to get them shortlisted, or at least firm up their place on that shortlist. A well-crafted CV that matches your top half-dozen strengths to the top six employer requirements will generally get you through to the interview stage. It gets your message across at the critical stage where you might be lost in a sea of hopeful applicants.

However, nearly everyone's job search would be improved if they did one thing: *they acted as if they had no CV.* For example, every time you're tempted to email a CV to start off a conversation, find another way of beginning that relationship. If you're approaching a recruitment consultancy you've heard good things about, you could simply email your CV across and see what happens. Alternatively, you could pick up the phone and ask for a conversation about a real job advertised at the moment.

Similarly, if there is one particular decision-maker you want to meet, sending a speculative email with your CV attached *might* work if your skills are in high demand. Most likely your approach has the same fate as every spam email received that day. In this case a speculative phone call might also be a high risk strategy – this is one of those occasions when you start to get your network (real and the virtual version in LinkedIn) to work for you, spotting someone who can connect you with someone who knows your target person, or at least the organisation.

So, use your CV for the purpose it is designed for: **to match your evidence to the requirements of a real job, in order to get you into the interview room.** Otherwise don't rely on it as a door opener, and don't allow it to become a conversation killer.

Other job search tools in your kitbag

Speculative approaches

Don't underestimate the value of a well-targeted speculative approach: sending a CV to an employer who is not advertising at the moment but who might need your expertise. This requires desk research, combined with good judgement about making an approach. For example, you might network your way towards a senior staff member, using LinkedIn to find people working at the organisation who can provide useful information. If you have no obvious points of connection, you might try pitching a speculative letter (see Chapter 15, pages 164–8), ensuring your attached CV is written in language the employer can buy into.

Responding to advertised positions

Even in a highly competitive market it makes no sense to rule out job advertisements, whether they are in print, online, or on an organisation's own job board. It's highly likely that you will need to adapt your CV in response. However, once your CV is in good shape you'll probably only need to make small adjustments, such as adjusting the flow of bullet points, or revising the language describing your experience.

Analysing job advertisements and job descriptions – eight vital steps

1 Look at the **order** and **weighting** of information presented in job documents. The opening requirements and those

given most space are your big clues about the top value items on the employer's shopping list.

2 Pick out **skills** required and think about range and level (see Chapter 8 on naming, measuring and framing your skills, page 89).

3 Study the **language** used by the organisation in its website and documents, not just about the job but in the way it describes projects, activity, and success.

4 Work out **where the job fits** in the organisation's structure, ensuring CV language matches the seniority of the role.

5 Pick up **key phrases** from the job advertisement and elsewhere and use them (sparingly) in your cover letter and possibly in your CV.

6 Spot desired **personality** characteristics and make sure that your CV examples show how your working style matches.

7 **Ask around** – cross-check what you learn from research against feedback from contacts who know something about your target employer.

8 Above all else, **research the organisation as if you were about to invest in it**. Look at brochures, reports, the website, but also talk to people who can answer the question 'what are they really looking for?'.

Interview problems arising from your CV

Too many candidates assume that an interview will be entirely about your CV history. In fact, some interviewers will make very little reference to it (and won't have read it in any depth). Others will go through it almost line by line.

To anticipate interview questions arising from your CV, think about positive and negative elements. Where you have presented positive facts that strongly match the job, an average interviewer may simply get you to talk them through. Avoid using the same words you used on paper; repetition bores the listener, so tell the stories in fresh terms, and have

new ones you haven't used up your sleeve. Positive information may also prompt probing questions: *what exactly did you
do? What were you, personally, responsible for?*

Negative information in a CV is a bigger problem. This
might be the wrong information, or the lack of it. It may
rule you out, or may lead to some very uncomfortable questions. So look brutally at any gaps or problems in your CV.
If there is something important missing, don't simply hope
for the best – include compensating evidence in a covering
letter (for example, if you lack a specific qualification, talk
about experience which has given you a similar knowledge
base). Negatives may also be things you can delete. Ask yourself 'what material might keep me off a shortlist?'. If you've
secured an interview, ask yourself 'what things in my CV
might this employer still be worried about?'.

For a comprehensive overview of interview preparation see
my book *Job Interviews: Top Answers To Tough Questions.*

Key points from this chapter

- ✓ Use all channels in your job search, but give
maximum time to the ones likely to give you
maximum results.
- ✓ Research and exploration are really important before
you get bogged down in the detail of a job search.
- ✓ Your CV will be important at various stages, but not
your sole way of gaining attention.
- ✓ Resist the temptation to send off a CV instead of, or
after, a meeting.
- ✓ Learn how to analyse what organisations are really
looking for, and provide a matched solution.

3

The essentials of a knockout CV

This chapter helps you to:

- Understand how your CV will be read by a busy employer
- Learn from other people's mistakes
- Take out the things that irritate recruiters
- Shift your CV above the average

> *'What is written without effort is in general read without pleasure.'* Samuel Johnson

Where and why CVs fail to deliver

On message, on time

Most CVs are written as if they were documents to be read in depth, like business reports. However, your CV may be skim read in 15 seconds. What other kinds of documents do you spend 15 seconds reading? Fifteen seconds is about the time you would spend reading a magazine advertisement or a poster. You give more attention to the cornflakes packet.

Strong CVs say what they need to say quickly, without fogging a simple picture. Many people have a sense that only half their CV works. The problem is, they're not sure which half.

When your CV is read an early half-decision is made. This process is similar to the way we form first impressions about people. If someone walks up to you in a party you decide instinctively if you want to engage in conversation – based on a range of clues (appearance, accent, tone of voice...). Something parallel happens when your CV is read. It's a complex response – which is a good reason why you can't fix your CV simply by downloading an Internet template.

An informed CV anticipates the **cold read**; in other words, working out how a busy decision-maker who knows nothing about you will react. Anyone reading over a hundred CVs is going to have to find a way of sifting through them very fast. You may think that an interview is just a conversation, but it's expensive to put professional staff into a room all day - so organisations need to pick out likely winners based on a paper sift (also known as 'pre-selection' or 'top slicing') – skim-reading for key phrases or pieces of information which earn candidates a place on the interview shortlist. In our CV survey one busy HR manager wrote: 'Tell me what it is that I need to know in as concise and as easily readable format as you possibly can in order that I can make sense of your CV. If I am scanning around 500 CVs for a role, my first-pass filter of them is measured in seconds rather than minutes.'

Grabbing attention, not just inviting it

Here's an example of an unfocused CV that isn't getting great results:

Avoid spelling mistakes (see the spelling of Curriculum Vitae and Driving Licence).

Don't title your document 'Curriculum Vitae', which makes you appear very old-fashioned

Don't overcomplicate your name

Use an email address you check at least twice a day, but **avoid** flippant sounding email addresses which communicate frivolity.

Don't include a date of birth, your age, or a National Insurance number. Don't refer to your nationality if you are British or entitled to work in the UK. No need to mention a driving licence unless it's a job requirement, and **don't** offer uninvited information about children or dependants.

There's no need to give titles to CV sections whose function is clear, such as the profile. **Avoid** a profile that is too limiting (for example by starting with your main qualification), vague and full of empty adjectives. Remember that the first phrases you use often pigeon-hole you in the reader's mind – so 'Modern Languages graduate' misleadingly suggests someone who probably wants to use languages in her career.

Avoid CV clichés such as 'dedicated' and 'hard-working'.

Avoid giving early prominence to your qualifications unless you are looking for a role where they are a strict requirement. Only list A level grades if you feel they matter (they usually don't if you have postgraduate qualifications). Don't list GCSEs or refer to results as 'passes'.

```
                    Curriculum Vitea

        Deirdre ('Deeds') Ann Prospect

    Address:      mobile:   09876 43210
    26 Random Street   home:     01235 67890
    Anytown       email:    slapmonkey@madmail.com
    X15 2GF

NATIONALITY: British
DATE OF BIRTH: 14/04/79
Full Driving License
2 children aged 8 and 10

PROFILE:
A hard-working and dedicated Modern Languages graduate with over ten years
experience in research, both academic and commercial. Aiming to exploit
existing skills and develop in new directions.

EDUCATION:
2000-2001  MPhil, Sociolinguistics
1997-2000  BA (Hons) 2:1, Spanish with Linguistics
1997       A-Levels: B,C,C,C
1995       GCSE passes: 5 A, 3 B, 1 C
```

List your best evidence early in the CV (avoid the term 'key skills').

State your role and the name of the organisation clearly.

Avoid vague summaries which mean nothing to someone who hasn't seen your work in context. Make it clear what you did, and what level your skills were used at.

When mentioning IT skills give examples which indicate your level of competence.

Avoid listing 'So What?' skills (see Chapter 12) – or skills well below your status, such as filing and photocopying.

Avoid vague, unimpressive terms such as 'office administration'. Write about specific tasks and what you achieved.

KEY SKILLS:

- M Phil in Sociolinguistics
- Project management and planning, including working to deadlines and prioritising
- Ability to work well individually and as part of a team
- Problem solving: using my initiative to resolve issues
- Excellent organisational and communication skills
- Experience of working with many different IT systems and applications
- Ability to work well under pressure

WORK EXPERIENCE:

Social Researcher, social policy research unit, June 2008 to May 2013. My role involved:

- Meeting clients in sponsor organisations (universities, local government and government) and designing research projects to meet their needs
- Developing research tools and carrying out interviews and focus groups
- Analysing and interpreting results
- Writing up and presenting results often for publication

My role involved extensive use of computer-based analytic tools and Microsoft Office, teamwork, organisation, working to deadlines and prioritising workload.

Office Administrator, Newtown Law, December 2005 to June 2008. Administrative position in a busy office environment. My role involved:

- Typing of witness statements and other court documentation
- Filing, photocopying, mail distribution and telephone enquiries
- General office administration
- Working as part of the typing office team and helping out as necessary

Administrative Assistant, Culture UK, London – June 2002 – March 2004. The role involved:

- Keeping records for the education resources section
- Corresponding with overseas offices
- Working with librarians in other countries
- General administrative and clerical duties
- Booking hotels for incoming conference delegates

Linguistics Tutor, New University, July 2001 – March 2002. I held a teaching position after completing my MPhil. My role involved:

- Teaching a weekly linguistics module for undergraduate students
- Lesson planning and preparation of materials
- Setting and marking of assignments and exam questions
- Individual student tuition

OTHER EXPERIENCE:

Postgraduate Student, New University, October 2000 – June 2001

To obtain my masters degree I carried out a major sociolinguistics research project involving investigations into dialect features in the south east of England. These projects required:

- Excellent organisational skills, effective time management and working to self-imposed deadlines
- Good written and verbal communication skills; the former in completing dissertations and the latter in presenting findings

Make sure you don't leave unexplained gaps, which worry employers. Even a busy recruiter will notice that there is a gap here between March 2004 and December 2005.

Avoid dull, predictable role summaries. Say something about why the role was interesting or challenging.

Do draw out transferable skills achieved from your education, but **avoid** blinding the reader with complex technical information or jargon.

If you don't hold training certificates in software, give concrete examples of what you have done with your IT skills. **Avoid** using vague terms like 'proficient', 'beginner' or 'intermediate'.

Avoid excessive use of bullet points and bold text.

Avoid listing interests which sound bland or half-hearted. List interests which might be relevant to a new employer, especially those involving work with other people.

Don't include the names of referees – you need to manage the process of when references are taken up. Also, these referees can help form an impression of your main focus – e.g. the two referees here reinforce the idea that this candidate is still looking for a role in the academic field.

- The ability to work under my own initiative to design research projects and materials
- The ability to establish rapport with a range of individuals of all ages in order to recruit them for the study and put them at ease in taking part
- The ability to work well under pressure to overcome problems

COMPUTER-BASED SKILLS:

- Proficient user of **Microsoft Office**, including **Outlook, Word, Excel** and **PowerPoint**
- Experience of analysis packages including **SPSS, NVivo8, GoldVarb and SNAP survey software**
- **Typing speed** 55 wpm

PERSONAL INTERESTS:

- I enjoy travelling and cooking.

REFERENCES:

Dr A Academic
Address Line 1, Address Line 2, Address Line 3, Tel: 01234 5689

Prof. Dr. B Academic
Specialist Institute, Address Line 1, Address Line 2, Address Line 3, Address Line 4, Tel: 01234 5689

Improved CV

This is the redraft of Deirdre's CV, ready to be market tested:

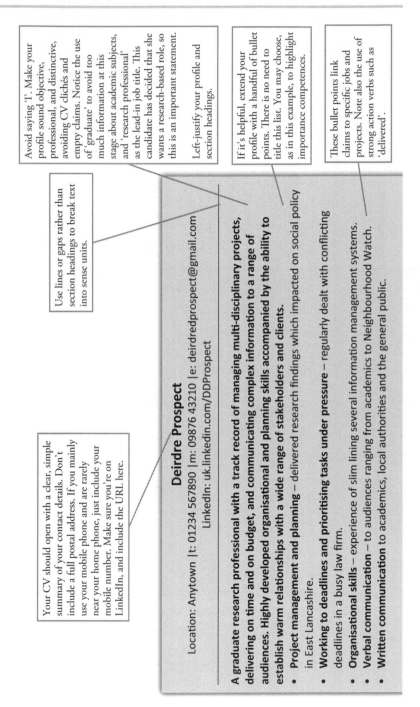

Avoid saying 'I'. Make your profile sound objective, professional, and distinctive, avoiding CV clichés and empty claims. Notice the use of 'graduate' to avoid too much information at this stage about academic subjects, and 'research professional' as the lead-in job title. This candidate has decided that she wants a research-based role, so this is an important statement.

Left-justify your profile and section headings.

If it's helpful, extend your profile with a handful of bullet points. There is no need to title this list. You may choose, as in this example, to highlight importance competences.

These bullet points link claims to specific jobs and projects. Note also the use of strong action verbs such as 'delivered'.

Use lines or gaps rather than section headings to break text into sense units.

Your CV should open with a clear, simple summary of your contact details. Don't include a full postal address. If you mainly use your mobile phone and are rarely near your home phone, just include your mobile number. Make sure you're on LinkedIn, and include the URL here.

Deirdre Prospect

Location: Anytown |t: 01234 567890 |m: 09876 43210 |e: deirdredprospect@gmail.com
LinkedIn: uk.linkedin.com/DDProspect

A graduate research professional with a track record of managing multi-disciplinary projects, delivering on time and on budget, and communicating complex information to a range of audiences. Highly developed organisational and planning skills accompanied by the ability to establish warm relationships with a wide range of stakeholders and clients.

- **Project management and planning** – delivered research findings which impacted on social policy in East Lancashire.
- **Working to deadlines and prioritising tasks under pressure** – regularly dealt with conflicting deadlines in a busy law firm.
- **Organisational skills** – experience of slim lining several information management systems.
- **Verbal communication** – to audiences ranging from academics to Neighbourhood Watch.
- **Written communication** to academics, local authorities and the general public.

EMPLOYMENT HISTORY

Social Researcher – Social Policy Research Unit June 2008 – May 2013
The role involved close liaison with sponsor organisations and the production of customised reports to assist with the development of community projects.

- Negotiated research needs with universities, and with local and central government.
- Designed customised research projects.
- Developed a range of bespoke research tools including structured interviews.
- Introduced focus groups to identify the perspectives of different stakeholder groups.
- Analysed and interpreted results for a wide range of audiences, including public meetings.
- Published in a range of outlets ranging from academic journals to national newspapers.
- Extensively used computer-based analytic tools, and Excel and PowerPoint to communicate numbers in a visual, exciting way.
- Mastered analysis packages including SPSS, NXixo1, GoldBarb and Acme survey software.

Office Administrator – Newtown Law, Dec 2005 – June 2008
Hired to manage the head office of a city centre firm of solicitors specialising in criminal law.

- Detailed checking of witness statements and other court documentation.
- Updated and redesigned five different information management systems.
- Produced complex typed documentation to tight deadlines.
- Undertook in-depth background research for Partners.

Break as homemaker – March 2004 – Dec 2005

Use section headings sparingly where they help the text make sense. Again, a line across the page is a useful design effect.

Embolden just the job title. Don't use bold text on the right-hand side of the page.

Include a short summary of each organisation and role, then a series of bullet points outlining your major achievements in each role.

Include details which tell the story of each job. Reveal enough detail about the role to show the level of difficulty of the tasks you undertook.

Note the consistent use of the past tense.

Be open and clear about gaps in your CV as far as you can.

Administrative Assistant – Culture UK, London   June 2002 – March 2004

Worked in the educational resources section of the UK's flagship arts and cultural organisation.

- Kept accurate records of books, journals and video material on loan to overseas offices and libraries.
- Consulted with overseas colleagues to meet a wide range of needs and demands, matching items to required language levels and cultural fit.
- Undertook all administration required in a busy department including financial records.
- Planned a 200-attendee conference, including all accommodation and travel arrangements for speakers.

> Reveal what inspired or impressed you about past employers.

Linguistics Tutor – New University   July 2001 – March 2002

Employed as a seminar tutor after completing my MPhil (research-based Master's degree)

- Planned, designed and delivered a weekly linguistics module for undergraduate students.
- Supervised and coached students on their research plans.
- Set assignments and assessed student work, including examinations.
- Provided one-to-one student tuition and learning support.

> Indicating the reason for career or study choices shows that you have thought about your career and made active decisions.

Postgraduate Student – New University, Oct 2000 – June 2001

Decided to take an MPhil in order to focus on the field of sociolinguistics (the way language plays an important part in society and community).

- Carried out two in-depth research projects into dialect features in the south east of England.
- Developed excellent organisational skills and effective time management in order to maximise interview time and meet deadlines.

> Explain qualifications, courses of study or specialised jobs if they are likely to seem impenetrable to the average reader.

- Communicated effectively in writing and verbally to a wide range of audiences.
- Planned and organised my own workload.
- Designed new research materials including a detailed interview.
- Demonstrated the ability to establish rapport with a range of individuals of all ages in order to recruit them for the study and put them at ease in taking part.
- Quickly learned how to solve problems under pressure, often re-arranging research interviews at short notice.

QUALIFICATIONS & CONTINUING PROFESSIONAL DEVELOPMENT

MPhil: Sociolinguistics, 2001
BA (Hons) Spanish with Linguistics, 2.1, 2000
A-Levels: English, Spanish, History, General Studies

ABC Statistical Training 2011   **GoldBarb User Training 2009**
Team Leadership 2009   **Communication Skills 2009**

INTERESTS / VOLUNTARY COMMITMENTS

Keen traveller (photography in Andalusia, India and Morocco). Exploring Thai cooking.

Annotations:

List qualifications and dates towards the end of your CV **unless** they will be instrumental in getting you an interview. Don't waste bullet points on this evidence, and put training courses in the same part of your CV.

Embolden your main qualifications and put a date against them. Use a two-column format if you have several training courses to list rather than use up valuable lines.

If your interests are not directly related to work, at least make them sound interesting and make your commitment to them sound active.

A CV containing this level of detail should not run over two pages. Avoid page numbers or any kind of header or footer because this breaks up the white space – about 2.5cm/1 inch all round looks good.

Out and out blunders

Do watch out for unintentional humour that bites back at you. One employer reported: 'Just received a CV today which included a photo. The individual was overweight and talked in his first paragraph about significant "expansion experience".'

In our CV research we asked HR specialists to give us examples of the typos, howlers, and unintended comedy that creeps into CVs. Here's a selection of lines from actual CVs:

- 'I always apply myself 10% to everything I do.'
- 'In all my previous roles I have been inellectually challenged.'
- 'As duty manager with XXXX Hotels I have a wealth of experience of customer complaints.'
- 'I left the country and unfortunately returned an older and wizened person. I could go on but I intend to write my own book.'
- 'Wholly responsible for two failed financial institutions.'
- 'I pay meticuououls attention to detail.'
- 'I worked as shelf stacker in a supper market.'
- 'Hobbies: I enjoy eating pizzas.'

Key points from this chapter

✓ Your CV is read at speed and decisions are made early in the process, based on front-end information.
✓ Avoid dull, unhelpful information which limits your options or sends out the wrong message.
✓ Interview-winning facts need to be presented early on page 1.
✓ Avoid other distracting information on the first page.
✓ Check the document carefully for errors which might rule you out.

4

Cataloguing your material

This chapter helps you to:

- Pull out useful evidence from your memory
- Translate and abbreviate your work history
- Build a database of information as a foundation for your CV
- Begin to communicate evidence of your skills

> *'You write to communicate to the hearts and minds of others what's burning inside you. And we edit to let the fire show through the smoke.'* Arthur Polotnik

Building a CV from the bottom up

Few CV books start right at the beginning telling you how to get your experience on paper. Remembering things you did some time ago may be tricky. It's often difficult to know what is relevant or what to leave out. You may worry if you have anything to say at all.

It really is best not to start by adapting a CV you wrote years ago. It's far better to start afresh. Few of us have the toughness to really edit our own material. However, before you start drafting a CV, do something else first.

Creating a CV data bank

Start with an unedited catalogue of your experience. Create a new document on your computer titled '**CV data bank**'. Don't use columns or tables – basic text will be better for cutting and pasting later (save time by using the same font style and size you will use in your CV).

If you remember better by holding a pen in your hand, begin a notebook full of CV evidence. Carry it with you on journeys and jot things down as they come to mind. If you're just as happy doing this on a screen, use a laptop, iPad, or phone to record ideas as they surface. Begin with the end in mind: several A4 pages filled with notes, bullet points, and short summaries.

This process is helpful for a variety of reasons:

- You will re-familiarise yourself with past events, which takes the strain out of job interviews.
- You will amass more information than you need, allowing you to pick and choose for a strong CV.
- You will identify good back-up examples for those times when you need to give examples at interview of things you haven't already detailed in your CV.
- You will start a process of re-engaging with your past which will help you write *and* talk about it with enthusiasm.

Facts and dates checklist

To make life easier later on, include facts and dates in your **CV data bank**.

Work history

Prepare a one-line summary for each job undertaken, for example:

Job title	Name of employer	Start date	End date
Sales assistant	ABC Promotions	May 2012	to date
Sales advisor	ABC Holdings	April 2009	May 2012
Trainee sales assistant	ABC Holdings	2005	2009

Ensure job titles and organisation names are completely accurate. It's usual to state the month and year you started and finished for jobs in the last four years or so. With older jobs you can generally just include the start and end year – see the example CVs in this book.

Qualifications

Remind yourself where you studied, the year in which you obtained each qualification, and the grades achieved. If you have A levels or above you don't normally need to list GCSE results, but it is probably useful to dig them out anyway just in case this information is needed. Type them into your 'CV data bank' file as follows:

Institution, name of qualification, grade/class, year completed
BSc Biochemistry, New University, 2.1, 2010
Diploma in Marketing, Newtown College, 2012
A Levels, Newtown Sixth Form College, Mathematics (B), History (A), Economics (C), 2009
Nine GCSEs at grades A–C, Hightown Secondary, 2006.

Learning history

Now would be a good time to find the documentation that lists the names and dates of training courses you have attended. As you discover them, record them as follows:

Name of training provider, training course, duration, year
Acme Training, Interpersonal Effectiveness, two days, June 2010
In-house training including: Writing Press Releases, Producing Podcasts, PowerPoint.

Product, project, and other organisational details

Forgotten the name of that project you led or that product you developed? Find it now, well before you try to finalise your CV. Sometimes you'll need to draw on old emails or letters (assuming you still have access to them), otherwise you may have to find archived brochures, reports, and other documents still in your possession. If you were not allowed to hang on to these documents when you left previous roles it might be useful to draw on the memories of work colleagues to fill in the gaps.

Other evidence

When compiling the evidence of your achievements outlined in this chapter, you may need to draw on facts and figures. This might therefore be a good time to put your hands on diaries, work logs, or any other documents you have which might, for example, provide details about sales or profit figures.

The great value of this approach is that it avoids the most common CV mistake. Your first instinct may be to describe personality traits (*'A highly motivated team player who ...'*). Building up hard evidence keeps the issue of your working style in the background at this stage – facts and details are going to be more helpful in building up your data bank than adjectives. By trawling your memory you get a much stronger grip on what you achieved, not what you think that says about you. Employers buy into experience.

Accessing your memory vault

Build up as much material as possible. Don't filter, edit, or leave things out because you think they're not useful. Give attention to non-working activity including study, hobbies, and volunteering. Two important rules apply:

- **Rule 1, put everything in** – don't worry about whether it looks or sounds relevant or impressive, just include it.
- **Rule 2, don't worry about wording** – as each memory comes to mind, just write down enough short phrases to ensure that the experience is firmly logged. You can decide how to present the evidence when you draft your CV.

It's important that you don't set the quality bar too high. As soon as people start thinking about successes and achievements they often think of things like climbing Mount Everest. Good CV evidence will usually be much simpler stories about tasks completed and challenges overcome.

At this stage don't worry about putting information in date order. The best approach here is *not* to write a methodical job-by-job history. You get better results by writing down evidence randomly, as it comes to mind, using the **Memory jogger checklist** below. Use the questions to help you remember specific events, projects, and experiences.

Memory jogger checklist

- Where have you acquired new skills or knowledge?
- Where have you faced a problem, obstacles, or a challenge?
- Where have you re-organised something?
- When have you done something that others said would be very difficult or impossible?
- Where have you come up with a new strategy or approach?
- Where have you delighted a customer?
- Where have you drawn on inner resources and surprised yourself?
- Where have you redefined a job?
- Where have you delivered more than expectation?

- Where have you invented new solutions or thrown out the rule book?
- Where have you gone the extra mile?
- Where have you turned near-failure into success?
- Where have you made a mistake you learned from?
- Where have you made connections from your learning or previous experience into a job?

Your aim when producing this checklist is to produce a sequence of short sentences, so your first page of notes might start to fill up like this:

- Zenith Project, 2005?, took over under difficult circumstances, got customer involved, beat implementation deadline.
- Learned to manage SAP interface on work purchasing system.
- Coached graduate trainee in supervisory skills.
- Gained 2.1 in university degree in difficult year – death of close family member.
- Found original material for university dissertation by conducting personal interviews with key economic journalists.
- Fundraising for Scouts international project 2011.
- Self-taught user of Photoshop and Lightroom.
- Level 2 Kayaking achieved in uni canoe club.
- Student job – re-organised restaurant booking system.
- Latest cost reduction exercise – made recommendations which saved 25% on outsourced IT contracts.
- Published article on student finances in the *Leicester Mercury*, July 2008.
- Trained in team leading and crisis management – mountain rescue service.

Selecting from your raw material

Your **CV data bank** is meant to be raw, unfiltered material, so whatever you write down should stay in your master document – it may be more useful than you think. Once you have spent a few hours trawling the recesses of memory for examples and cross-checked against work diaries, earlier versions of your CV, and the memory of your partner, friends and colleagues, you can start to edit.

When you feel your master file is fairly complete ('fairly complete' will do – you don't need to catalogue everything), you can then start to think about the information you will lift out to place in your CV. Don't make changes to your original 'CV data bank' file. Save a copy of the file (for example, called 'Edited CV raw material') and keep the master file untouched – it will be useful to you later in your career to help you remember details.

Don't worry if there are blanks or gaps – this document is simply a memory prompt. Keep adding things as you remember, and keep collecting information from all the sources available to you, for example conversations with former work colleagues, or friends and family who remember something about your work history.

Editing by theme

There are several useful ways of reviewing and managing your evidence at this stage:

- Group pieces of evidence together so they relate to particular jobs.
- Highlight pieces of evidence that should be fighting for space at the top of page 1 (see Chapter 12, page 124).
- Colour code your evidence to identify themes (for example, related skills).
- Highlight the material you think might be most relevant to your next job move.
- Sort your evidence into work and non-work categories.
- Look for gaps where you need more evidence or facts to support statements.
- Highlight evidence which needs clearer or punchier wording.

Editing by content

Soon you will start to edit and filter so that you have text ready to paste into your CV. Most of the time this information will end up in bullet point form, so it makes sense to start to adopt that style now. Go through your notes, translating longer sentences into bullet points which adopt the style you will use in the CV itself (see Chapter 8). Keep things concrete. If the bullet points don't sound exciting yet, don't worry – you can edit them later.

Your aim at this stage is to filter down so you have got about two A4 pages of bullet points. As stated above, you might group these by themes or by job. For example, your original file note might state:

```
Set up task group (found members, formed group, led
meetings). Needed to look at possibility of placing
all accounting functions in one site in Cheltenham.
Result - £50K centralisation project signed off and all
completed on budget within 5 months.
```

Adapted into a short, punchy bullet point mentioning the name of the company this now reads:

■ Formed and led a task group to plan and executive £50K project to achieve a centralised accounting function at XYZ Packaging.

Edit down your material into strong bullet points like this. You will probably end up with more material than you need, but that's not a problem. When you compose your CV you will be able to choose (a) which bullet points end up highlighted in the first part of page 1 and (b) which points you will use in the job-by-job section of the CV.

The process of filtering down is important. Think of it this way. Imagine you are an artist with hundreds of paintings stacked in your studio. You're pitching for a major bursary, but you can only present 12 paintings. You begin with hundreds, get it down to under 50, and then you will decide on your final 12. Finally you decide on the one representative painting that you would like to go on the cover of the publicity flier. You select, refine, and limit so your best work comes to the forefront.

Skill sampling

While cataloguing your material you might find that you are making notes about what happened rather than what *you* did. Dip into your **CV data bank** and pick half a dozen or so examples of projects which you think might reveal *skills that are relevant to the kinds of jobs you are chasing*. List those projects in the **skill sampling grid** below.

Skill sampling grid		
Draw out six or so strong items from your CV data bank. Analyse them as follows (make up your own grid or download an A4 copy – see page xvi).		
CV data bank item	**What did I actually do?**	**What skills was I using?**
e.g. Document scanning project	Training three temp staff	Planning; communication; leadership; supervision; organising workloads
Report summarising consultant expertise	Gathered information on consultant expertise, qualifications, and specialism	Interviewing; consulting; data management; report design; report writing
Crisis budget	Drafted revised budget in 2011 in relation to loss of grant income	Consulting with senior staff and colleagues; data collection and checking; negotiating; communicating difficult news

| Mentoring graduates | Mentoring two or three new graduate entry staff per year | Mentoring; coaching; reviewing; setting goals; summarising; encouraging |
| Presentation to conference 2010 | Gave talk on managing change in a large organisation | Planning; negotiating; communicating; using visual aids; using humour and analogy to communicate; networking |

See Chapter 8, pages 89–91, for more on recording your skills.

Step-by-step processing

It might also help to look at one or two of the stronger achievements identified in your **CV data bank**, and to think through each stage of activity as follows:

- Planning and anticipating
- Action – what you did
- Dealing with unexpected snags and problems
- Your impact on others
- The result
- What you learned from the experience.

You are almost certainly *not* going to spell out this level of detail in your CV, but it's great interview preparation, anticipating probing questions about your experience.

Avoid rehashing old job descriptions

Zoom in on specific projects: the shorter the timescale, the better the detail. A weak CV might end up saying 'managed a range of information gathering projects', activities which took place over several years. A better summary is focused and concrete: 'Set up a pilot data management project for ABC Bank in 2010, consulted with key stakeholders, moved to nationwide implementation within 6 months.' Generalisations wash over us like a vague cloud; specifics stay in the memory as tangible evidence. Too many CVs simply describe the role in the same terms used in the original job description. Notice, for example, the difference between this draft job summary line:

```
Client services co-ordinator - Aardvark Lighting,
2011-2012
Responsible for handling all incoming telephone and
email enquiries, sending out brochures, answering
customer questions.
```

and this improved CV item which moves away from the basics of the job and starts to show what the candidate did to change the role and make a contribution to the organisation:

Client services co-ordinator – Aardvark Lighting, 2011–2012
Handling all incoming enquiries for a supplier of high quality reading and work lights:

- Helping customers understand their needs and matching them to the right product range.
- Providing technical information, or connecting customers with technical experts.
- Translating general enquiries into customer relationships.
- Recommending and introducing a new Customer Relationship Management system.

Key points from this chapter

✓ Build up a catalogue of evidence from scratch.
✓ Trawl for good stories which reveal your skills, achievements, and strengths.
✓ Don't start editing down until your raw material is fairly complete.
✓ Don't try to shape it into CV language too soon.
✓ Look at themes to start to get a sense of your career story.
✓ Begin to turn material into bullet points.

5

Choosing the right CV format

This chapter helps you to:

■ See the advantages and disadvantages of different models
■ Appreciate the downside of a functional CV
■ Understand why a profile may be useful
■ Anticipate the impact of different CV structures on readers

> *'Form follows function.'* Louis Henri Sullivan
> (American architect)

Does it matter which format I use?

Beware of any guide that suggests there is a perfect CV structure. What matters most is this: what a winning CV looks like to your target employer. What format and phrasing are going to grab the attention of a decision-maker? You get the answer to this question from a variety of sources: recruitment consultants, employer websites, work colleagues, industry contacts, people who have been hired recently. Once you know what information your target employer hopes to see, feature it on the first page of your CV – whatever structure you use.

Don't make the mistake of choosing a CV format (a) because it looks easy or (b) because it's close to a format you've already used in the past.

Problem formats

If a CV isn't working at all it's probably because it emphasises the wrong information on page 1. It's probably one of these five variants, the last two of which we will discuss in detail:

1 A format which wastes opening lines on irrelevant personal details, as discussed in the example CVs in Chapter 3, pages 25 and 30. This biographical approach distracts readers; in some CVs this information takes up a third of page 1.
2 An ego trip: a document that makes more of a statement about **personal qualities** than experience.
3 A CV which is essentially a series of **chopped-up job descriptions** (see Chapter 4, pages 45–6). Your CV says what the job required, not what you did and how you added value.
4 A CV which gives too much attention to your **qualifications and study history**.
5 A **functional CV** which lists skills and competences without providing a clear job history.

The **qualifications-led CV** is understandable. If you have spent three or four years achieving a degree, you naturally want to say something about it. However, by communicating the idea that your study is the most important thing about you, you encourage an employer to believe you might be happier remaining in academic life. Equally, unless your qualifications are directly related to the jobs you're applying for, you may be sending the message 'I have no experience, but great potential'. This is unhelpful to employers because it's back to front – work information is hidden on page 2 (and skills may not be brought out at all).

Employers *are* interested in your qualifications, and if you have worked hard and done well these qualifications are worth listing and celebrating – but not as item 1. Draw out aspects of your studies that will be interesting to an employer:

- Why you chose the course of study.
- What you got out of it and how you believed it would enhance your career.
- Obstacles overcome and skills acquired during your studies.

Simply doing some bridge thinking between your studies and the world of work can lead to an above-average CV.

The functional CV – use with caution

If you have ever tried to switch from one work sector to another in a very different field, you'll have discovered that it's not easy. Sometimes, just your past job titles and the language you use to describe your skills is enough to communicate a lack of suitability, and you may find it difficult to persuade a new employer that your skills are transferable. Transfers to and from the private, public, and not-for-profit sectors often create such problems, but you can experience difficulties making any kind of move between fields of work, for example from traditional manufacturing into a high-tech industry.

Attempting to make a sector change relying on your CV alone is a struggle. Your evidence works against you. In a tight market, employers become more conservative – they look for candidates who have done a similar job in a similar organisation. Employers skim-read your CV looking for matching job titles and names of familiar employers. Recruitment agencies are often even more conservative, and if you send them a CV that doesn't offer the sector experience they seek, you will often receive no feedback at all. Their focus is often on one item – your most recent job title.

If you have faced this problem in the past, you will have come to the conclusion that a conventional CV listing your job history is a poor tool for effecting a transfer between sectors. You may have been recommended to write a functional CV. This avoids listing a job history at all, and instead sets out skills and competencies that closely match target jobs.

The example below shows you how the first page of a functional CV might begin. Page 2 will often be either a further list of skills and competencies or might be a conventional, job-by-job list. The CV is for someone who wants to move from a public sector service role into a private sector sales position. As a result, she is trying to overcome her lack of private sector experience by pointing to useful skills, for example, business development, customer care and budgetary management. She has also been careful to adopt private sector terms, for example, 'accounts', 'customers', 'orders' rather than 'partners' and 'contracts'.

Below is an example which looks good at first glance but may receive market resistance.

Example functional CV – page 1

Name
Contact details

Profile
A results-focused graduate professional with a history of success in initiating and guiding projects, event management and creating measurable improvements in customer service standards. With extensive experience of liaison with a range of external partners in both the private and public sector, now seeking a business development role in a flexible, forward-looking organisation.

Business development skills
Built strong relationships with key accounts, solving quality and ordering problems, and adding extra value - resulted in a 27% increase in department orders, and four major new external customers won in the last 18 months.

Planning skills
Planned, organised, and hosted a regional conference for 200 colleagues. This involved planning the programme, booking speakers and the venue, and organising invitation letters, delegate packs, and follow-up documentation.

Customer care skills
Using highly developed customer-facing skills, responsible for handling customer complaints to our department and have also planned a proactive programme of client consultation to gather information about the level of customer satisfaction in our top 40 users. Designed and wrote a new customer service handbook.

Budgetary management
Responsibility for setting and agreeing departmental budgets and reporting on actual versus budget costs on a monthly basis.

Functional CV – health warning

The functional CV looks great as a concept. Some coaches still recommend it and CV services still produce them. It's a model which majors on skills and communicates the fact that they are transferable, and offers linked achievements meaningful to an employer in a new sector. So why should it be used with caution?

The first problem is that if you pick the wrong skills or describe them in a way that doesn't match the job, you waste the format. A much bigger problem is that nearly all recruitment agencies and a great many employers have taken a strong dislike to functional CVs, largely because it's difficult to establish where and when you worked, because skills are presented out of context, and because it looks like you're trying to conceal your work history or lack of recent employment.

CV formats that work

The profile-led CV

We now turn to a CV format that is generally acceptable to employers (as the Appendix demonstrates). This CV kicks off with a short summary paragraph – a profile. The profile-led CV is far harder to write than a straight-in CV because it's difficult to write a good profile (see Chapter 11).

The main reason for writing a profile is *explanation*. If you were handing across a CV in person it would only need to be a work history. If you were in the room saying 'here are some things I'd like to tell you before you read a word of my CV', you'd only need a basic document. Of course, most times your CV is read you will be absent and won't be able to provide a verbal introduction. The document needs to work on its own.

If it's perfectly clear what kind of role you'll be going for next, based on your work history, then a straight-in CV is all you need. If your CV needs a handover or a 'before you read further, know this …' introduction, it needs a **profile**.

A typical opening profile for a graduate in her mid-20s might look something like this:

> Commercially minded individual with extensive experience of developing business and working within a sales-driven environment. Experience of leading the marketing and sales department in a big city marina/leisure complex builds on a former track record of achievement in the hospitality sector. Now seeking a private sector role where strong customer relationships and quality are prized.

The final sentence would of course be taken out if this candidate was using the CV to chase a specific job.

A profile may stand on its own, or might be followed very swiftly by a short set of related bullet points. There is usually no need to give a title to this list, or to your profile. So a more senior candidate's profile might say:

A versatile chartered chemical engineer and manager with experience in a wide range of technical, operational, and leadership roles. Well-developed management and influencing skills with a history of leading effective teams. A strong track record of project management including commissioning and managing a new plant, with a sound technical understanding of all areas of process plant design and operation:

- Technical lead on a new Chinese manufacturing plant, 2012.
- Led a management team to scope out the acquisition of ABC Industries – project completed ahead of target.
- Commissioned and supervised new web-based technology support system, 2011.
- In-depth understanding of health, safety and environmental legislation and responsibilities.

Advantages of the profile-led CV	Disadvantages
■ Your CV begins with a paragraph that summarises who you are and what you have to offer ■ The profile may include evidence about what makes you distinctive ■ If you have had a variety of jobs it becomes easier to focus on what you want to do next ■ Your most recent job can still be spotted quickly	■ Profiles are not always popular with recruitment consultants ■ If badly written, the profile sets a poor tone for the whole CV ■ If you have had a variety of jobs it's not clear what you want to do next ■ The wrong opening description can push you into the wrong kinds of jobs ■ Achievements may become disconnected from the jobs to which they relate

You will find examples of profile-led CVs throughout this book.

The straight-in CV

This CV format gets straight into your work history. After setting out your name and contact information, the first piece of information is your most recent job, followed by the rest of your job history. The CV generally concludes with a section on your learning history and information about your outside interests. It's plain, uncluttered, but has both pros and cons.

Advantages of the straight-in CV	Disadvantages
■ It gets immediately to your most recent job – assuming that this is your main selling point ■ It is popular with recruitment consultants ■ Your CV will almost certainly be no longer than two pages ■ Jobs are presented in a clear order ■ It is clear which skills you used in a particular job	■ If you fail to translate job responsibilities into active information about skills and achievements the CV will be ineffective ■ You may be put in the wrong box – pushed into an identical job to the one you have just done, with little opportunity for new learning ■ If you have had a variety of jobs it may not be clear what you want to do next

The idea behind a straight-in CV is that jobs speak for themselves. They don't. You need to explain them, unpack the tasks involved, and show what you achieved. Don't describe every aspect, but pick the top achievements in each role and list them as bullet points.

When should you use the straight-in CV? Where you don't need a profile. For example, if you're looking for the next obvious role in your sector. It's a no-brainer, no-fuss approach that says 'this is what I do know, and I am in the market for the next job up the ladder'. The fact that it is straight-in makes it popular with recruiters; it's also the kind of CV you might use for seeking a promotion.

Career coach Stuart McIntosh takes the robust view that 'a straightforward, simple and honest reverse chronological CV, preferably without a profile, is the recommended option for those seeking a similar role in a similar sector. In the main, recruiters favour a no-nonsense, no bells and whis-tles approach to CVs, and unless you are seeking to reinvent yourself then simplest is best.'

Where using a straight-in CV with agencies, ensure you have a detailed conversation about the job you want next – what seems obvious to a recruiter might be wrong for you. You might want a sideways move to gain different experience, or the same role with an organisation that has alternative values or a different culture.

For details about how you can download an example straight-in CV see page xvi.

Still thinking about which format to use? The next chapter outlines how to choose a CV format to match your personal situation.

Key points from this chapter

✓ Be aware of the pros and cons of different formats.
✓ Anticipate employer responses to the format you choose.
✓ Go for a format which communicates what you want to say.
✓ Focus on the impact of page 1 material.

6

Structuring your CV to match your circumstances

This chapter helps you to:

- Match your career stage to the most useful CV structure
- Appreciate how choice of format can help you overcome market barriers

> '... inside every old person is a young person wondering what happened.'   Terry Pratchett

A CV that matches your needs

The CV you need varies according to the career stage you have reached. The list of contexts below is not exhaustive, but for each stage the most useful format is outlined. Each case assumes that you get the basics right (appropriate use of page 1 material, identified skills and achievements, plus evidence which is focused on the needs of your target employer).

School leaver

Most school leavers' CVs focus too much on educational history. Your qualifications are important, but you're better off going straight into your work history (of any kind) rather than background information. Avoid huge claims you can't justify. List skills acquired from your study, work experience, or extracurricular activities (especially team experiences). This CV may be a single page. (See also Chapter 13, page 143, for CV tips to help those leaving full-time education.)

Seeking an internship or short-term assignment (paid or unpaid)

A one-page CV can work here, with a similar emphasis on work to the school leaver CV. The million dollar question here is: why you? Most others applying for the same internship will have achieved qualifications on a par with yours. First emphasise what makes you a good candidate, and secondly what attracts you to the opportunity. Demonstrate a valid career reason for choosing the internship.

Where you have little work experience

This will probably be a single page CV, but you need to work hard to demonstrate where you have learned and used skills. Work with a friend to draw out evidence of your skills, from any part of your life. Capture skills acquired from your hobbies or interests outside work. List any kind of work experience, including temporary work, voluntary work, vacation jobs, or work placements. Write about what you did rather than the context.

Staying in the same sector, but moving on to a more demanding or interesting job in your chosen field, or seeking a promotion

If the job you're after is an obvious step up, emphasise how you have already acquired skills and accepted responsibilities above your pay grade. Include evidence of where you stepped in for someone more senior, took initiative, supervised others, or took difficult decisions. A CV which clearly outlines skills and achievements will generally put you in the frame for this kind of role.

Wanting to move from routine jobs into a more professional role

Your profile is going to have to work hard here, capturing the range of sectors and roles you have worked in and emphasising skill levels (see Chapter 8, page 89) and achievements. As with the promotion model above, you'll need to demonstrate where you have used skills to a high level (see Chapter 8 on naming, framing, and measuring your skills). Rather than looking like a disconnected list of jobs your CV should tell a story of skill development. Include evidence of sector or job knowledge, for example by writing about your learning.

College or university leaver seeking first permanent job

If you include a profile, consider simply using terms such as 'graduate' or 'qualified' unless your qualification is directly related to the work you're chasing. You can then detail your qualifications later (you probably don't need to list GCSEs unless specifically requested), and make sure the first half page emphasises any kind of work experience or contact, including all temporary jobs, vacation jobs, work placements, internships, and work visits. Give a strong emphasis to work-related skills.

Think about the support skills you can offer, and an employer's expectations (for example, IT, word-processing, customer service, or sales skills). Indicate your standard of competence. When outlining your qualifications, translate them into terms that the reader will understand (drawing out your transferable skills). Make sure you include interests, as they will often communicate a rounder picture.

Same sector, seeking second job after graduating

Two pages maximum, probably largely composed around a straight-in CV model unless you want a very different role in the same sector. If you state a target job, make sure it's not over-ambitious. Include good detail about your first job, including linked achievements and previous work experience.

New sector, seeking second job after graduating

This CV should be no more than two pages. The format depends on whether you want to change sector or carry on along the same path. If there is no obvious link between your degree subject and your first job then use a profile to gain leverage. Make clear links between your studies, your previous experience, your present job, and your ideal next role. Detail what you learned and achieved in your first job.

Returning to work after taking a study break to obtain a postgraduate or professional qualification

Your most recent qualification is part of your main message, but not the whole deal. Begin with a well-written profile that explains briefly why you chose to return to study, what you learned from it and how you hope to apply it in your next role (or promotion). If you want to emphasise the breadth of your career, consider a **career summary** (see Chapter 7, page 76).

After a long and difficult job search

The format depends on whether your likely next role is predictable or you want to do something new. The main focus should be on skills and where you have used them – it may be the lack of such evidence in your CV that has failed to get you shortlisted. Make sure that your primary message is not about your job search or being unemployed. If there is a clear gap between the present date and your last job, list activities you have undertaken (including study, training, volunteering, and organisation visits).

Returning to work after a career break

Use a well-crafted profile to capture your work history and to indicate where your career is heading next. Emphasise work-related achievements early to firmly suggest that this is your main focus. Suggest that you chose to take a career break for positive reasons, and be prepared at interview to talk about the barriers you had to overcome to make it happen – and what you got out of it. Show how you make your own life decisions and learn from them. Do remember that an employer is wondering if you are now fully committed to a return to a more 'conventional' working pattern, so emphasise your commitment to a long-term role.

Returning to work after a gap taken for personal or family reasons

Use the career break model above, and deal with the 'personal issue' briefly. Honesty is the best policy. If you have been away from work for more than two years, introduce evidence of skills exercised in the intervening period (for example, in voluntary work). Don't give the reader any indication that your skills are out of date (avoid putting dates against training courses you did some time back). If your reason for having a gap was to do with family responsibilities, be very clear about your current availability.

Wanting to stay in the same role but in a different sector

This CV will inevitably be profile-led. Give a value reason for wanting to change sector, and say what experience, know-how, and skills you want to bring across. If you have spent a long time in one sector it is best to leave job-by-job details until page 2. Emphasise your skills more than the organisations you have worked for. Sector knowledge can be emphasised in the profile or possibly in a career summary.

Wanting to stay in the same sector but in a different role

A profile-led format will probably be required, as here, once again, you have to sell a particular idea to a recruiter. You will probably need to take the emphasis off your main qualification and your professional background. You may also find that it helps if you focus on relevant training. When discussing your work experience take the emphasis off your previous job titles. Give enough concrete evidence to show that your skills are transferable. Include evidence from projects or placements where you have gone outside your job description. The biggest emphasis of all (probably in the profile, but consider a career summary) should be on (a) your in-depth knowledge of the sector and (b) your clearly articulated motivation to stay in the sector but in a new role.

Wanting to change role and sector – to do something completely new

This is the hardest kind of CV to write. Your profile has to work overtime here, spelling out your reasons for change, what attracts you to the new role and something of what you have to offer. Give particular emphasis to (a) clarity of purpose and (b) saying something distinctive and unusual about your background – tickling the reader's curiosity is often what gets you through to a first interview. Work hard at communicating your transferable skills rather than just listing them.

Applying for a role that has defined competencies

Your target employer may publish a list of detailed competencies for the job. Match your evidence carefully, structuring your evidence to match the listed competencies, giving concrete examples. Often a cover letter works better than a CV as a method of doing this. You may have to dip into your study, personal interests, voluntary work, or other life experiences to find matching evidence.

Wanting to get into a new, highly competitive sector

This CV needs to be no longer than two pages, with a profile that suggests two or three reasons why an employer might want to meet you even though your background is unconventional. Something distinctive and unusual (including multi-sector experience or a career break) might get you noticed. Remember that a CV is far less likely to give you breakthroughs than a well-planned programme of networking.

Trying to get an interview for a job where you have little obvious experience

Use a CV profile to take the emphasis off your work experience and previous job titles. Work hard on your profile and your linked achievements, and also explain and sell your transferable skills. Make sure your profile gives a clear, motivated reason for wanting to make this kind of move. A career summary might help bring out useful background jobs. The odds are long on this kind of application, but if you can get into the interview room you have a chance. Again, a multi-strategy job search involving plenty of people contact is vital.

Age 50+ and finding it hard to get an interview

If your CV looks smart, modern and includes an email address you're already moving forwards. Don't provide endless information about jobs you did over 15 years ago. Major on up-to-date transferable skills and recent evidence of achievement. Get a younger colleague to check the language – are you using terminology that a 25-year-old recruiter would find archaic? Don't include your date of birth, the age of your children or anything else that overemphasises your age. For the same reason, you may want to avoid a career summary as it may overemphasise your length of service. Do include recent work-related projects if you've been unemployed for a while.

Wanting to find a permanent job after a series of temporary positions

Emphasise your broad range of skills and experience; you may have experience of a wider range of roles and organisations than people who have stayed in one role for years, and you should be able to point to a good range of transferable skills. The problem is that your CV can look very transitory, and can be mistaken for the CV of someone looking for another temporary job. Your first task here is to make sure that your list of temporary jobs has an overall shape. You might, for example, group jobs together and summarise a series of roles as one block of work. You will need to demonstrate how the variety of your work experience has been a good preparation for working in a permanent role. In your covering letter and at interview communicate clear reasons why you want to work for one employer for the next stage of your career. Don't be afraid of including the phrase 'seeking a permanent role'.

Looking for a temporary or contract job

A one-page CV may suffice. Don't worry about the profile or the complications of communicating the idea that you want a permanent job. An agency needs to see (a) a skills summary, (b) a list of roles and organisations for the last two to three years, and (c) your main offerings in terms of qualifications and training. Skills and achievements are everything – an agency wants to know if you can hit the ground running. An indication of availability is often also welcome – how far are you prepared to travel and how soon could you start a new assignment?

Seeking work as an interim manager

Interim managers are typically hired to cover relatively senior positions for anything between a month and a year. A proven track record in a particular sector is going to be a must, so a career summary may help. An interim management agency will usually need to see a fully developed list of skills. Describe your work history in terms of projects you started and completed, and mention the names of past employers or partner organisations. Emphasise project management or change management skills. Include as many relevant keywords as possible that would be required by your specialist area.

Key points from this chapter

✓ Spot the scenarios which most closely match your situation.

✓ Learn how to use a CV format to help overcome difficulties you may face.

✓ Begin with this advice as an overview of the shape your CV needs to take.

✓ Draw on other chapters as you begin to work on CV content.

7

The mix & match CV

This chapter helps you to:

■ Understand the benefits of a mix & match CV
■ Communicate your strongest messages on page 1
■ Learn how to pitch and position achievement evidence
■ Decide whether you need a career summary

'Innovation is creativity with a job to do.'   John Emmerling

Layout leads to impact

As the previous two chapters have confirmed, you have choices in the format of your CV. You might go for a straight-in CV, which is simple and unfussy. If you're relatively happy in your work and just looking for greater responsibility or a change of scenery, a straight-in CV may suit you perfectly.

However, a straight-in CV is a poor tool if you want to move into a different line of work. Agencies are all too eager to categorise you, and you'll inevitably be offered jobs which repeat your current role. The second problem with a straight-in CV is that an employer has to read through two or three job summaries to work out your sector experience and the range of skills you possess.

In a profile-led CV, the alternative, your profile has to work hard to get every point across, and isn't the place to list all your skills. A good profile is short and punchy, and if you try to overpopulate it with evidence of how and where you used skills, and list achievements, it'll be too long.

The solution? Cheat. Take the best of all structures and combine them in a hybrid format.

The mix & match CV

The strength of this format is this. By taking the best aspects of the profile-led CV and functional CV, this model gets key information on page 1 in this order:

- Simple, short **contact details** (see Chapter 12, page 124, on fine-tuning page 1).
- An overview of who you are and what you have to offer – your **profile** (see Chapter 10, page 107).
- (Optionally) tagged on to the end of your profile, a short number of bullet points – your **profile plus** (see Chapter 11, page 119).
- **Job-by-job information** including a clear statement of your job title, the nature of the role, and bullet points cataloguing achievements (see Chapter 8, page 81).
- A quick summary of your relevant **qualifications** and learning history (this may appear on page 2).
- (If it's helpful, an at-a-glance overview of your work history – a **career summary**, discussed below.)
- Enough page 1 information to persuade someone to check out page 2.

To summarise:

Features in a mix & match CV	
Required on page 1	**Optional on page 1**
Abbreviated contact information	Profile plus – summary bullet points immediately after your profile to capture your career highlights
Profile	Details of qualifications
Most recent job title, summary of the role, and a detailed set of bulleted achievements	Career summary
Bullet points summarising evidence of achievement against additional roles which fit on page 1	Roles before your present job

Example mix & match CV

There's no need to title your document Curriculum Vitae – it looks very old-fashioned. Print your name as you wish it to be used at interview

Horizontal lines rather than section headings to separate content

Clear, brief contact details including an email address

Alison Nameless

Location: Newtown | m: 06777 654321 | e: arn1@example.com
LI: uk.linkedin.com/AlsNameless

An experienced graduate communications professional with a track record showing well-developed powers of persuasion in speech and writing. With a background in HR and people development, experienced in designing and implementing in-house communication solutions and transforming employer brands:

- Designed and delivered a comprehensive communication programme across all group companies during a merger transition period.
- Managed a team to re-design and deliver a 'new-look' group website.
- Designed and managed the roll-out of a Europe-wide corporate identity programme.
- National Student of the Year for CIM exams.

Lead with job title on left, followed by organisation name and dates of employment

Separate each section clearly

The **profile** is a short paragraph summarising *relevant* parts of your background. It sets out the main experience, skills and know-how you want to offer an employer. It can be supported by a shortlist of strongly related bullet points, particularly if you are looking for a change of direction

EMPLOYMENT HISTORY

Communications Manager – Nicetech   Nov 2012 to date
Responsible for setting and rolling out policy regarding internal communications, and for managing an in-house communication team.

- Designed, co-ordinated and delivered a comprehensive internal communication programme across all European locations.

- Introduced a European Newsletter – sourced business, technical and human-interest stories from nine European sites, organised translation services.
- Initiated, designed, and implemented a new group-wide company staff development Intranet.
- Designed and conducted UK-wide staff training programmes.
- Member of the Site Executive Management Team responsible for managing an HR team, providing a comprehensive generalist HR service supporting 300 people.
- Negotiated and established a group-wide Intranet and communications policy.

HR/Communications Assistant – Nicetech, Newtown   2010–2012
Responsible for launching and editing an in-house
magazine.

- Established and managed production of a global company magazine.
- Initiated a communications programme reaching out to 13,500 staff across Europe.
- Introduced a site-wide Team Briefing process – ran training sessions for managers.

Internal Communications Assistant – Chocolate UK   2007–2010
Looked after in-house communications for this large confectionary
manufacturer.

- Organised and managed a very successful Royal Visit to open our new site.
- Produced a 'diary-style' video of the preparations for, and the actual Royal Visit.
- Organised groundbreaking ceremony and Public Relations activities for a multi-company training initiative.

HR & Communications Manager – Giant Telecoms   2003–2007
Responsibility for all HR activities including: recruitment, remuneration,
'downsizing', employee relations, performance management, training and
development.

- Launched a management development programme leading to Investors in People (IIP) status.
- Researched, designed, and implemented a 'shop floor to top floor' pay and grading system.
- Designed and introduced a competency-based appraisal and recruitment programme.

HR Assistant – Giant Telcoms   2001–2003
- Undertook a wide range of HR duties with a growing emphasis on internal communications.
- Completed CIPD qualification by examination.

QUALIFICATIONS, CPD

History BA (Hons.) 2.1, Manchester University 2001
CIPD, City College 2003
Handling the Media Course 2010   **Photoshop CS4 2011**
Presentation Skills 2009   **Personality Profiling (SHL) 2005**
Management Skills Programme (ABC) 2005

> Group training with qualifications in one clear-to-view section

INTERESTS / VOLUNTARY COMMITMENTS

Hill walking, kayaking, trustee of local disability charity and improving my spoken Italian.

> Include interests that might be relevant to the job, those that indicate co-operative or team working, or simply things you can talk about at interview with enthusiasm

Here's another example of a mix & match CV for someone in their second job, this time in a slightly different style with material grouped together in themes:

James Steady
Location: Maintown | m: 06777 654321 | e: james1@steady.com
LI: uk.linkedin.com/JamesRSteady

Commercially minded individual with extensive experience of developing business and working within a sales-driven environment. Experience of leading the marketing and sales department in a big city marina/ leisure complex builds on a former track record of achievement in the hospitality sector:

- Designed and negotiated a successful local radio advertising campaign leading to 40% increase in customer enquiries and 25% increase in turnover in 2012.
- Developed a working partnership with a range of high-end goods suppliers.
- Assisted in the planning of the Maintown Music festival weekend, attracting 2,000 visitors and 60 local bands in the course of one weekend. Undertook negotiations with a range of official sponsors including XXX and YYYY plc.
- Developed a deal between AAA magazine and Central, where the magazine held a large-scale two-day networking event during a major political conference.

EMPLOYMENT HISTORY

Head of Marketing, Central Leisure Complex   Jan 2009 – May 2013
Role covered a mixture of marketing and sales management duties for Central.

- *Marketing* – developed marketing strategies for Central via both direct and indirect marketing. This involved developing a strategy, communicating budget plans to senior management and gaining agreement, then delivering a marketing campaign on budget, providing weekly updates on costs and outcomes. Planning, managing and analysing marketing campaigns and providing a final cost/benefit report.
- *Sales* – identifying opportunities to bring in new business to the leisure complex. This involved maximising sale for Central and ensuring team members were aware of sales targets and driving the team to guarantee targets were met. Building relationships with local businesses, customers, and community through various public relation events. Building a large database of corporate and customer contacts and ensuring they were aware of any sales promotions.
- *Advertising* – designing advertising campaigns for events held within the Marina and negotiating with external agencies, local and trade press over cost and terms of adverts placed. This has covered

traditional advertising campaigns via print and radio to more modern media like social networking sites such as Facebook, Twitter, and LinkedIn, as well as the use of search engine optimisation. Agreed and developed advertising packages in the regional press.

- *Events* – creation and development of events held within the marina complex, this included agreeing a budget with superiors and ensuring the event ran within budget guidelines, was commercially successful and delivered what was required. Organised a range of successful events ranging from charity nights, special dinners, and large corporate events.
- *Finance* – ensuring that on a daily basis Central's cash takings tallied with the onsite sales management system and processing company. Setting up a new system to link financial and sales records. Analysing marketing spend maximising revenue. Experienced user of Sage Online50.

Assistant Manager, Mainville Wine Bar & Restaurant,   2006–2007
Assistant Manager of busy suburban bar while
completing studies.
- Successful completion of personal licensee certificate.
- Ensured the smooth running of a successful bar, dealing with customer complaints, and difficult customers, and staff problems.
- Checked and maintained stock levels, checked deliveries, and reconciled stock and cash.
- Opening and closing the premises when the manager was on annual leave.
- Planning rotas and dealing with sick absences or late arrivals on shift.
- Ensuring cash takings co-ordinated with the in-house sales management system. Sage Online50.
- Processed employee time sheets and holiday records.
- Effective time management – holding down a responsible position while studying.

QUALIFICATIONS, CPD

BTEC National Certificate in Property Management, Mainville College, 2007
Areas of study included: investment appraisal, applied valuation, property marketing and PR.
Certificate in Hospitality Operations (2008)
A Levels: Geography, Sports Studies

INTERESTS/VOLUNTARY COMMITMENTS

Five-a-side football, skiing, half marathons, training for the North East Triathlon next year. Travel in South-east Asia.

Can I avoid writing a profile?

The profile sets out your stall, and draws immediate attention to the things you want an employer to notice. The profile is so important it gets a special focus in Chapter 11, pages 118–23. It should be the last thing you write when drafting a CV. If you try to write it straight away you will very probably get stuck or dispirited, and it will be difficult – largely because you haven't yet got a complete overview of your work history.

In the mix & match CV the profile must be focused, free of flowery adjectives, and in a language targeted at the right decision-maker in the right organisation. All listed achievements should link to hard evidence and, where possible, should indicate where you were working when you used the skill.

Adding achievement evidence to page 1

As Chapter 4 outlined, once you start to build up evidence of past achievements you begin to see certain themes and patterns emerging, and you get a sense of the pieces of evidence you want to give special emphasis. If they don't naturally appear on page 1, you may have to consider using the profile plus model outlined in Chapter 11, pages 119–21.

Getting achievement evidence across isn't about listing, it's about getting the minimum information across in the right language. Turn to Chapter 9, pages 94–106, for detailed advice about how you capture achievements.

Qualifications, training, and continuing professional development

It's optional whether a *brief* summary of your primary qualifications appears on page 1 or deeper inside your CV. The only question is whether the information is likely to get you shortlisted (see Chapter 12, pages 124–133, on sharpening up page 1).

The optional career summary

A career summary should be used with care, and only if it's useful.

The idea of the career summary is that it presents your entire work history at a glance – useful if you have worked in a range of well-known organisations, or if you want to demonstrate you have experience of a range of sectors. So, for example, here's page 1 of Alison's CV with a career summary added and more prominence given to her qualifications:

Alison Nameless
Location: Newtown | m: 06777 654321| e: arn1@example.com
LI: uk.linkedin.com/AlsNameless

An experienced graduate communications professional with a track record showing well-developed powers of persuasion in speech and writing. With a background in HR and people development, experienced in designing and implementing in-house communication solutions and transforming employer brands:

- **Designed and delivered a comprehensive communication programme across all group companies during a merger transition period.**
- **Managed a team to re-design and deliver a 'new-look' group website.**
- **Designed and managed the roll-out of a Europe-wide corporate identity programme.**
- **National Student of the Year for CIM exams.**

> Note that qualifications now appear on page 1, which also includes a career summary

QUALIFICATIONS, CPD

History BA (Hons.) 2.1, Manchester University 2001
CIPD, City College 2003
Handling the Media Course 2010   **Photoshop CS4 2011**
Presentation Skills 2009   **Personality Profiling (SHL) 2005**
Management Skills Programme (ABC) 2005

CAREER SUMMARY

Communications Manager	Nicetech Pharmaceuticals	2012 to date
Internal Communications Manager	Chocolate UK	2007–2012
HR and Communications Manager	Giant Telcoms	2003–2007
HR Assistant	Giant Telcoms	2001–2003

EMPLOYMENT HISTORY

Communications Manager – Nicetech   Nov 2012 to date
Responsible for setting and rolling out policy regarding internal communications, and for managing an in-house communication team.

- Designed, co-ordinated, and delivered a comprehensive internal communication programme across all European locations.
- Introduced a European Newsletter – sourced business, technical, and human-interest stories from nine European sites, organised translation services.
- Initiated, designed, and implemented a new group-wide company staff development Intranet.
- Designed and conducted UK-wide staff training programmes.
- Member of the Site Executive Management Team responsible for managing an HR team, providing a comprehensive generalist HR service supporting 300 people.
- Negotiated and established a group-wide Intranet and communications policy.

HR/Communications Assistant – Nicetech, Newtown   Mar 2010 to Nov 2012
Responsible for launching and editing an in-house magazine.

- Established and managed production of a global company magazine.
- Initiated a communications programme reaching out to 13,500 staff across Europe.
- Introduced a site-wide Team Briefing process – ran training sessions for managers.

The major disadvantage of a career summary is that it can draw attention to the fact that you have spent a long time with one employer.

When would you use a career summary?

- When you want to draw attention to previous roles on the first page of your CV.
- When you can show a clear history of progression and promotion.
- When you can list several well-known organisations.

- When it is helpful to show experience in a range of roles or sectors.
- When you have achieved above-average progression.

When should you probably <u>not</u> use a career summary?

- When you have been with the same organisation for a long time (although it is still worth considering if you have undertaken a wide range of roles, so you are demonstrating that you have enjoyed a career inside one organisation).
- When you have problem gaps in your CV.
- Where you have changed jobs very frequently.
- Where your career history looks like an unconnected series of roles.
- Where you have limited work experience.

Improving layout to gain reader impact

My colleague Kate Howlett is an expert on the visual layout of CVs, drawing on a range of recent research including the F-shape reading model (Western eyes read documents and web pages in an F-shaped pattern – twice horizontally, lines near the top of a document, and then vertically, scanning the left-hand edge).

Kate suggests that 'your CV format should do everything possible to draw the reader's attention to the most important parts of the document – and at the same time avoid irritation. Avoid using a header or footer or page numbers – anything which detracts from the symmetry of the page and sense of blocks of information floating in white space. However, most employers *do* like profiles – in the age of Twitter we like bite-sized information.'

Here are Kate Howlett's top tips for writing your CV:

- Symmetrical design at the top of your CV always appeals. Centralising your contact details is a popular style, but left-justify remaining text so you get even gaps between characters and words allowing for 'speed reading'.

■ Set your margins at 2.5 cm if possible so it doesn't look like you've crammed as much as possible on to two pages.

■ Make sure your document is A4 size – too many people use the default 'Letter' size which will print off unevenly.

■ Use a clear, modern font which looks good on screen, for example, Calibri (no smaller than 11.5pt – small print makes readers feel angry with a document).

■ Don't repeat sub-headings, for example, 'achievements/responsibilities' as it draws eye time away from more important information such as job titles. All your responsibilities need to be expressed as achievements.

■ Only use bold print on the information you want read in 20 seconds – the average time a reader will spend on your CV. For example, use bold to emphasise key words near the beginning of a line.

■ Group similar items together. If you have separate sections for 'Qualifications' and 'Training' the reader will usually skip one of them. Be careful not to include too many sections – each new section forces the question 'should I read any further?'.

■ Ensure consistent use of the third person in the past tense (for example, 'Organised ...').

■ Don't worry if a list of bullet points breaks between pages – better that than a large white gap at the bottom of the page.

■ Use line spacing and dividing lines carefully to lead the reader's eye into the next part of the document (see example CVs in this book).

Completing your mix & match CV

Starting at the bottom of page 1, include your job-by-job details as outlined in Chapter 8, pages 81–2, with a few bullet-pointed achievements against each role (half a dozen or so for recent roles, cutting down to two or three for roles you did some time back).

The layout of the first page should be uncluttered. Think of it as attractively laid out blocks of information. Career coach Ruth Winden writes: 'Enjoy the white space you created. Your readers will thank you for it.'

Key points from this chapter

✓ Be aware of the limitations and problems of functional, straight-in, and profile-led CVs.
✓ Exploit the advantages of the mix & match model.
✓ Structure your page 1 evidence so that the reader sees vital information first.
✓ Learn how to communicate achievement evidence and details of your qualifications and learning history on page 1.
✓ Consider whether a career summary is helpful to you.
✓ Think carefully about layout and impact.
✓ Start sub-headings and bullet points with information-carrying words.

See page xvi for details of how to download further CV examples.

8

Constructing your job-by-job history: turning events into evidence

This chapter helps you to:

- Write effectively
- Identify and communicate your strongest skills
- Attach tangible achievements to each role listed
- Adopt the smart third person
- Communicate evidence as well as claims

'It is by acts and not by ideas that people live.'   Anatole France

Starting at the back

Most people try to start writing a CV from the beginning. This is the toughest approach. Would you try to write the executive summary of a report before anything else? Capturing your work history on paper is a process of turning events into evidence. You start with extensive raw material (see Chapter 4, page 41), and then begin to cut down that information so it makes sense to an employer.

A CV will contain about 50–60 details taken from a lifetime that spans thousands of events. Your job eventually is to filter these down so that your very best information is what hits the reader immediately. You will, however, find that you work out what gems to lead with by building up bullet points gradually, starting with jobs you did some time back. Here is an example:

Tourist Information Officer – Newtown Tourist Board, 1992–1995
Working in a busy Town Hall tourist centre dealing with telephone, walk-in, and email enquiries from the public.

- Understanding customer needs and providing matched solutions, including detailed journey plans.
- Selling a range of books and services including room bookings.

Use the same style consistently throughout your CV when detailing jobs, using four steps:

1 **Job title, organisation name, dates worked** (you might choose to lead with the dates). It might be helpful to mention the location of the employer (not the full address).
2 If the employer is not widely known, **describe the organisation** briefly – as in the logistics manager example below.
3 **Summarise the role** (ideally in no more than two lines).
4 Use bullet points to **list top achievements**. These can include acquired skills, knowledge, training, or important experiences. For a job you did some while ago, two or three bullet points will be enough, for your more recent role you may have six or eight.

So, for a more senior role:

Logistics manager – Abstract Cartons, Newtown, 1998–2000
Supplier of pre-packaged cartons to the food sector. Managed the factory distribution team, reporting directly to the operations manager.

- Managed a transport pool including LGV vehicles.
- Monitored all daily deliveries in the East Midlands area.
- Responsible for fleet maintenance schedule.

Write right

Let's not be too stuffy about CV English; most CVs use a rather clipped, abbreviated style and aren't written in complete sentences or perfect paragraphs. Even so, spelling, punctuation, or grammatical errors may immediately condemn the document to the 'no' pile. Most spellcheckers will pick up gross errors, but won't spot the wrong word. So if you type 'lead' when you meant 'led', or 'loose' when you meant 'lose' (two common mistakes) your computer won't see the difference. Proof-read carefully (try underlining each word as you read slowly, or reading backwards). Watch out for software that changes everything into American English – British readers tend to dislike US spellings (*center, labor, theater, color, defense*) and can be resistant to American-sounding terms even though they are acceptable spellings in British English (*realize, recognize, organization*).

Your computer may mislead you when it comes to punctuation. Watch particularly for rogue apostrophes (as in 'managed multiple project's' and incorrect use of 'its' and 'it's'). No need to take a class – just find the right person to proof check that your CV is correctly punctuated.

Use phrases that feel authentic for you – which usually means *using simple language*. Too often candidates use formal language because they think it sounds more impressive (for example, 'utilised', 'vacated', 'corresponded with') when shorter words work better (for example, 'used', 'left', 'wrote to'). 'Cut' is better than 'abbreviated', 'grew' better than 'maximised'. Most memorable slogans are composed in short words in everyday language. Saying 'no employee was ever terminated for purchasing from the IBM corporation' doesn't have the impact of 'nobody ever got fired for buying IBM'.

What's wrong with writing 'I'?

Career coaches used to encourage the use of 'I' in CVs for emphasis, showing that the candidate owned his or her skills. In today's market, should you use 'I' (the first person), 'he' or 'she' (the third person), or ignore both? Let's start with a statement written in the first person:

- In this role I set up a call centre function, operating
  on a shift working basis. This required me to negotiate
  with a wide range of staff and change the way claims
  processes were undertaken, and also to commission new
  IT systems to support the call centre team.

Here's a rewrite in the third person:

- In this role she set up a call centre function,
  operating on a shift working basis. This required her
  to negotiate with a wide range of staff and change
  the way claims processes were undertaken, and she
  also commissioned new IT systems to support the call
  centre team.

The bullet point is still too long, taking too much time to
set the scene. Both 'I' and 'she' make the text feel anecdotal
rather than hard evidence. The answer? As with the question
of choosing CV formats, if you're faced with options you
don't like, invent a new option. Many successful CVs are
written in a particular kind of third person which is largely
found only on CVs.

A punchy third person voice found only in CVs

Language specialists may have a term for it, but let's call it the
smart third person:

- Introduced a call centre function on shift working basis, re-engineered existing
  claims processes, and commissioned new IT systems in support.

Why does this tightened up version work? It is punchier
because the very first word is a verb. It quietly misses out the
pronoun, stating 'Introduced' rather than 'I introduced', or
'She introduced'. It also underlines the idea that this is a past
event – something complete, therefore successful. The 'smart'
version of the third person is a neat way of getting information
across without your CV sounding too personal, or too distant.
It guarantees that you cut at least one word per sentence and
start each bullet point with a word that makes a mark.

Building up your evidence

Simply listing jobs and responsibilities provides an average CV. To make your CV stand out, dig deeper for the information that really matters.

Your **CV data bank** (see Chapter 4, page 37) provides the building blocks, but don't be surprised if you remember equally useful examples while revising. Increase the number of bullet-pointed achievements as you get closer to your most recent job. So, for a job that appears part way down page 2, you still need to demonstrate achievements to show you added something to the role:

Membership Co-ordinator – Institute of Transport Professionals 2004–2006
Head of team managing membership function for professional body with international reputation. Responsible for organising membership database and handling member enquiries.

- Membership team praised in the ITP annual report for generating the largest number of innovations in 2011.
- Organised a migration of all records to a new software platform.
- Managed the transfer of 7,500 member records within 6 weeks, cross-checked for accuracy, with a measured 44% improvement in member satisfaction ratings.

Another example:

Senior Editor – Magic X Publications, Milton Keynes Mar 2004–Feb 2007
Magic X is the UK's largest publisher of self-help books focused on the magic/conjurer sector. The senior editor is responsible for editing the monthly magazine *Magic Matters* (circulation 15,000) and a number of annual booklets.

- Improved circulation from 9,000 to 15,000 in two years.
- Renegotiated printer contracts to cut annual production costs by 20%.
- Improved advertising income by 50% and rebooking levels by 22%.
- Secured a profile of the magazine on Switch TV's 'Look Out', March 2006.

Writing about your most recent job

Write about your current (or most recent job) in detail, because it is going to get maximum reader attention. This may be a problem if it's not a job you want to repeat, but it is one that the mix & match CV format outlined in Chapter 7 attempts to resolve. If the job before is more relevant, make sure that appears on page 1 as well.

Careers expert Zena Everett (www.second-careers.co.uk) has researched how employers and agencies evaluate CVs. This showed that recruiters often skip past the profile and go straight to the current or most recent job, reading on only if these details are of interest. Everett adds: 'Recruiters preferred short personal statements and recommended that job-seekers avoid waffle such as "works well individually or as a team" at all costs. The ideal personal statement should comprise a summary of the applicant's career to date, a statement of their career objective and a reference to the skills that bridge the two. The rest of the CV should back up the profile with evidence of the applicant's previous achievements. A really good statement, pulling the candidate's career history together, might have a mitigating effect on a weaker CV.'

An employer or recruitment consultant picks out a range of important information from your most recent (or current) job:

Information	Questions and concerns
Job title	The title may quickly convey what you're looking for next. The job title may be unclear, or may be the kind of job you don't want to repeat.
Seniority	Do you look senior enough? Is your experience at the right level? Is this communicated by your job title, responsibilities, and by the language you use to describe the role?

Name of organisation	Is it a 'blue chip' or household name? Will the name be recognisable? If not, how are you going to communicate what kind of employer this was? Have you mentioned the names of well-known organisations which the job brought you in contact with?
Role coverage	Do you convey the level of difficulty/complexity in the role? Is it clear what you were responsible for (people, spend, facilities). Is it clear what you added to the role?
Skills	Do you provide evidence to back up claims made about proficiency? Are the skills linked to tangible achievements? Are the skills described using the language of your target employer?
Achievements	Are they credible? How difficult were the challenges involved? Do they sound predictable? Are they varied in terms of outcomes? Have you gone beyond what was required of you? Are they described in language that excites your target employer?
Development on the job	What have you learned from the role? What training have you received? Have you kept your skills and knowledge up to date?
Length of time in post	Is this unusually short or long for this organisation/sector? Why did (do) you want to move on?

Therefore, the most recent job carries a lot of weight – it's often the first thing a reader examines. You will therefore say more about it than you have about previous jobs. Include five or six bullet points to give the job weight:

Customer services assistant – Example Tool Distribution   Sept 2011 to date
Team member in a busy call centre environment dealing with incoming enquiries
and problems for a large tool hire company.

- Dealt with a range of routine and complex enquiries within time constraints.
- Undertook outgoing calls to build up customer database – increased sector list
  by 40%.
- Capable of identifying and escalating priority issues.
- Produced detailed call logs and analytical reports.
- Mastered in-house software and Excel for monthly reports.
- Consistently beat monthly team targets for gaining customer referrals.

You might use up to 10 bullet points. If you have more than
six, it's wise to group them under sub-headings. For example:

Business travel consultant – AcmeB2B Travel, London   June 2010 to date
Acme B2B provides a bespoke travel service to the business community,
specialising in media organisations. Role based at the busy West End
branch.

Organisation skills
- Organised international travel arrangements for business customers,
  for groups and individuals.
- Arranged all delegate accommodation for 2011 Beijing Conference for
  Institute of Transport Specialists.
- Produced a report to Directors on prospective customer relationship
  management software.

Customer relationship management
- Dealt with all incoming enquiries in a busy West End office.
- Booked London accommodation for large group of Canadian news
  teams for 2012 Olympics.
- Bid for and won a new contract with a major media group worth £120K
  per annum.

Managing and developing others
- Designed and wrote 30-page staff induction module.
- Trained staff in telephone techniques and communication skills.

Providing skill evidence

Many people mix up skills with personality traits. For example, being 'outgoing' is an aspect of personality, but 'good at building relationships quickly' is about putting personality into effect using a range of communication skills. Skills are what we *do* at work. If someone was filming you from 50 feet away they would record mainly what you *do*, rather than what you are like. Of course, some intellectual skills such as analysing or lateral thinking only become obvious by the results you achieve.

Name, frame, and measure your skills

Communicate your skills on three levels:

1 **Name** the skill. This may take more care than you think. For example, 'managing stakeholders' might be very meaningful language in one sector and in another might signal your unsuitability.
2 **Frame** the skill. Set the scene by providing a context – where were you using the skills? What problem were you trying to solve?
3 **Measure** the skill. Make it clear what standard you have achieved. This is often made clear by giving an example of where you used a skill at the highest level.

Here's an example:

- *Negotiated* (**named**) *menu simplifications with our Director and Head Chef* (**framed**), *resulting in 25% improvement in profitability* (**measured**) *and reduced food waste.*
- *Presented* (**named**) *the findings of the engagement survey to the entire 300-strong workforce at ABC's national conference* (**framed**), *achieving above-average speaker rating from delegate feedback* (**measured**).

■ *Redesigned* (**named**) *ABC's sales handbook for 200 call centre staff* (**framed**), *receiving a personal note of thanks from the Sales Director* (**measured**).

Transferable skills

Many would agree with Kate Howlett that transferable skills are 'an urban myth'. They are widely misunderstood; many candidates believe that listing their skills is enough to make them transferable. Others assume that it's the job of an intelligent reader to make connections between your experience and the job on offer. The important principle is this:

> **An employer will only believe your skills are transferable if you communicate them in language the employer finds convincing.**

The only thing that makes your skills transferable is the language you use to describe them. How do you know what language to choose? A great place to start is to repeat or rephrase the terms used in job documentation. A secondary, but vital, strategy is to talk to people in your target sector and make a note of the language they use to describe high-performing candidates and successful outcomes. So, for example, if the role requires 'sensitive management of stakeholders', your CV is going to have to use that kind of language to get noticed.

The issue of how you make skills transferable is a particular concern for those moving between the public and the private sectors. Public sector language does not generally work well if you're transferring into a commercial environment, but it's equally true that the language of targets and profits may not work if you're seeing a social enterprise role.

Skills and challenges: checklist

Skills
Where have you learned new skills?
Where have you built on old skills?
Where have you chosen to apply your skills creatively?

People skills
Where have you developed people skills?
Where have you created, contributed to, or led a team?
Where have you managed or worked in a team which wasn't functioning well?

Learning
Where have you picked up specialist knowledge, for example, about products, systems, or software?
Where have you managed your own learning?
Where have you learned to do something difficult?
Where have you taught someone else, or passed on a skill?
Where have you received feedback or coaching which has changed you?

Projects
Where have you started, concluded, or adapted a project?
Where have you picked up a failing project?
Where have you succeeded against opposition or when you were told it couldn't be done?
Where have you completed something on time, on target, on budget?
Where have you beaten a target?
Where have you come up with ideas (or adapted the ideas of others)?

Role development
Where have you fulfilled all requirements of a job?
Where have you exceeded the requirements of a job?
Where have you helped redefine and extend a job?
Where have you deputised for somebody more senior than you?

Challenges

Where have you done something you were proud of?

Where have you been stretched?

Where have you done something you didn't think you could do?

Where have you changed direction for a good reason?

Where have you made the best of difficult circumstances?

Where have you built on mistakes or failure?

Where have you built on difficult feedback or criticism?

Projects

Where have you started or completed a project?

Where have you taken over a project started by somebody else?

Where have you succeeded against opposition or negativity?

Where have you completed something on time, on target, on budget?

Where have you beaten a target?

Impact

Where have you influenced, negotiated, persuaded, or sold?

Where have you passed on a difficult message?

Where have you communicated well verbally?

Where have you communicated well in writing?

Where have you delighted a customer?

Where have you added value or made a difference?

Go through this checklist once for paid work, then review the questions again thinking about other activity including volunteering, study, or leisure interests.

Key points from this chapter

✓ Start writing your CV from the back.

✓ Summarise the role and organisation.

✓ Use bullet points to capture what you added to the job or where you made a difference.

✓ Use the **smart third person** to achieve greater impact.

✓ Decision-makers pay close attention to your most recent job – give careful attention to what you say about it.

✓ Increase detail as you move towards your most recent job.

✓ Recognise your skills – and then describe them in language which works for your ideal next employer.

9

Writing about achievements

This chapter helps you to:

- Communicate your strengths briefly and effectively on page 1
- Manage bullet points and page layout carefully
- Edit your CV to filter out material that is obvious or too junior
- Monitor tone and express your personality on the page

> *'To achieve great things, two things are needed; a plan, and not quite enough time.'*   Leonard Bernstein

Telling the story in concise terms

The style you adopt in a CV is obviously not the same as talking about yourself. You have to put down words which work purely as text, without you there to unpack what they really mean:

Interview statement	CV statement
'The last time I led a team under difficult circumstances was when I set up a joint project planning group to deal with the merger. We dealt with a huge agenda and a big workload to integrate two IT systems. My job was not just to keep people focused but to encourage professionals from two very different organisations to work together.'	Formed a joint project planning group of key staff from both organisations: achieved goal of integrating data from separate IT systems and built a well-knit team.

In an interview you're forming a relationship; your CV on the other hand needs to convince through facts. Consider the following draft achievement statement:

```
Having looked at all in-house communication, I had the
idea of launching an in-company newsletter. I took the
idea to my boss, took responsibility to design a cover,
and wrote the text for a pilot issue. I had to run the
idea past the MD to get permission to print off copies
for all UK locations, so the newsletter went out to 644
people. I redesigned the newsletter two years later,
first of all as an attachment sent out by email, later
we organised an interactive email that allowed users to
click through to interesting pages.
```

This material is interesting and detailed – about the right length for a good interview answer, but too long for a CV – readers won't want to take the time to go through lengthy blocks of text. Nearly every sentence begins with 'I' (see Chapter 8, page 84, on using the **smart third person**). The above text includes phrases that sound repetitive ('I had the idea' ..., 'I had to run the idea ...'). It takes too many words to make each point. The long opening sentence runs the risk of losing the reader. The last sentence is even longer, and complicated by sub-clauses.

A revised bullet point looks like this:

■ Negotiated and launched UK-wide company newsletter (readership 600+). Designed and wrote all material in text and web-based versions.

Sharpen your bullets

Even though you have a little more leeway here than you do in the profile, it's important to be economical with language and make each bullet point count. Ask the question *what's the main point here?* The point is to show initiative, drive, or demonstrate a skill. You want to get this information across in a single bullet point, ideally one that will be only one or two lines long. Full lines against every bullet point looks like continuous text, which readers find less attractive, so vary bullet point length.

A CV turns a dull list of tasks into language which communicates energy. Energised language matters hugely in an interview, too, but there you can adjust speed, tone, and pitch of voice. In an interview you can probably say 'I am motivated by deadlines'. On paper those words sound like you're stating the painfully obvious.

In our CV survey employers repeatedly asked for clear, active language. Don't write 'A plan was established' (the passive voice); begin your bullet point 'Planned ...'. Plain English means shorter words. Don't write 'This activity led to the receipt of a design award', write 'Won a design award'. Wherever possible, claim the things you did personally. 'Organised' is fine. 'Helped to organise' is weaker – what was the extent of your participation? Twitter teaches us to communicate complicated messages in just 140 characters, so abbreviated language is within everyone's grasp.

Communicating energy on paper begins when you pick the right words to begin bullet points. Start with action verbs which convey enthusiasm, commitment, initiative, or decisiveness, for example:

Less active verbs	More Active verbs
Put together	Shaped
Contributed to the planning of	Planned
Administered	Organised
Supervised	Managed
Encouraged	Motivated
Arranged	Organised
Started	Initiated
Approached	Convinced
Started	Launched
Compiled	Wrote
Trained	Coached
Presented	Delivered
Participated in	Contributed to
Became involved with	Committed to
Began with difficulty	Kick-started
Took through	Steered
Discussed with	Persuaded
Agreed	Negotiated
Helped to grow	Expanded

Beefing up your evidence of achievement

In an effective CV skills are named, measured, and framed (see Chapter 8), but you need to link these claims to solid achievement stories. It's very common for people to be poor at spotting their own achievements, and many CVs fail to mention them at all, or make claims that sound unconvincing. A CV without clear statements of achievement is not worth writing. This evidence answers the question 'what happened because *you* were in the job?'.

Career coach Ruth Winden writes: 'Performance, achievements, impact – this is what recruiters look for. This is what your CV should focus on – not your duties or responsibilities. Everyone has duties and responsibilities, yet not everyone brings results. But it's the results that matter.' Kate Howlett's view is that many candidates push too hard: 'Don't consciously try to "sell" your experience, but record what you've done at work with clear metrics, for example, "Managed 11 staff over two UK sites".'

You may feel uncomfortable because of natural modesty, or because you're working in a sector that is suspicious of the language of achievement. You may feel that your work experience has been all about 'soft' skills which you believe are impossible to measure. Too many people fail to recognise what they have achieved. They often say '*I haven't achieved anything important*' or '*that's what everyone does*'. Those who are sensitive to their impact on others find it almost physically painful to come out with simple, assertive statements of their strengths. Here are some tips that will help:

- Start with the facts; look at your actual achievements.
- Write in the language that an extrovert boss in your organisation would use in describing what you have done.
- Imagine you are writing the description about someone else you admire and want to help.
- Enlist the help of someone good with words to describe your achievements.
- Recruit the help of someone more assertive than you to come up with stronger ways of describing what you have done.

■ Interrogate your writing for signs of excessive 'spin'. Would your claim stand up to probing questions?

Career coaches spend so much time saying 'blow your own trumpet' you'd think we were frustrated brass players. Overdone modesty just doesn't work in a CV. In the usual 30-second dash through your CV a busy recruiter just doesn't have the time to put two and two together. If your CV says that you were 'involved in restructuring the accounts department' it says very little. If you meant that you initiated and pushed through the most radical changes in your department for a decade, then say so. You don't need to be unique – being distinctive is enough.

Offer concrete evidence

Here's a draft set of achievements from a sales-focused CV:

Business development
Developed a new set of clients in a previously unexplored industry sector and created business opportunities for my company.

Client servicing
Maintained customer accounts and provided professional support to individuals and companies on their recruitment needs.

Interviewing skills
Interviewed and pre-screened candidates to assess their fit to job openings available with clients.

Sales and marketing
Achieved sales targets through a customer-focused approach by attracting assignments from key customers on an ongoing basis.

Training and development
Conducted relevant HR courses at management school.

Several elements need tightening up. Hard evidence is required against several achievements. 'Developed a new set of clients' and 'created business opportunities' could be transformed into 'built £n worth of new business'. Employers could be named (this candidate in fact worked for one of India's largest recruitment agencies, and built extensive business with blue-chip companies). The last point about training and development is vague, sending out the opposite message to the one intended – at the moment it sounds a little like 'I've done at least one course vaguely related to HR in a college you've never heard of, and I am reluctant to say if I finished the course.'

More advice from Keith Busfield: 'Cut the crap. Get the red pen out. Use the dying art of précis wisely so every word, comma, and semi-colon adds value to the message.'

Real outcomes

Outcomes frame achievements. Careers specialist Stuart McIntosh writes: 'I am amazed at how few achievements *are* actually achievements as they fail to show a measured outcome, for example, *Developed a new engagement strategy for the organisation which was adopted across the company*, this seems to stand up to the classic challenge of "so what?" but on further scrutiny one hasn't got a clue what the actual effect was.'

Therefore, if you are applying for a more senior role you need to give examples of achievements which look good, sound good, and actually convey something. Look, for example, at the bullet point below:

- ```
  Developed a new engagement strategy for the
  organisation which was adopted across the company.
  ```
  ```

To an expert reader this claim makes sense and sounds effective, but doesn't convince as something that reveals enough hard facts to show that something tangible was achieved, so:

- Developed and gained Board agreement for a staff engagement strategy. New metrics introduced which revealed a 15% improvement in engagement scores across the business.

Look for energy, not just words

Struggling to find the right choice of words? Abandon them for a minute or two. Go back to the experiences you are thinking about and remember how they *felt*. Ideally talk to someone about these times when you were highly motivated and completely focused. When you've talked about them, write down the words you used. This helps you to communicate that original energy. The art of writing down achievement stories is all about retrieving the feelings behind the facts.

This strategy also encourages you to **show rather than tell** – don't tell someone you're a great organiser, reveal it through your evidence. Stories communicate far more clearly than bare information.

Watch the left-hand edge

Recent research has looked at eye movement in a CV reader. For example, research published by TheLadders (www.theladders.com) used an eye-tracking technique to analyse how online CVs are read. The findings included the idea that recruiters spend just six seconds on their initial decision about whether a candidate fits or not, largely based on key data points which include organisation names, current job title, previous position, start and end dates, and education history.

Career coach Kate Howlett reminds us that: 'only 7% of the population actually read anything. The rest of us scan-read. Our eye line follows certain areas of the page which means that we should put the most important facts in our CV in the key areas of the page and go with the natural eye flow.' These methods are consciously used in advertising and explain why certain parts of a newspaper page are more expensive to advertise in than others.

Eye flow theory suggests that readers fix very briefly on certain zones in the text – often the areas that are highlighted in some way or in bold print. In a CV we are attracted to headings, sub-headings, section breaks, and bold text – so use them where they provide most value. Remember that readers are also attracted to text on the left-hand side of the page – begin bullet points with strong verbs.

Below you can see examples of bullet points taken from various jobs within two CVs. They use active verbs and the **smart third person** (see Chapter 8):

Example 1: achievement bullet points for a managerial CV

- Managed an engineering support facility for XYZ Ltd with a repairs and maintenance budget of £95K per year.
- Budget holder and cost centre manager delivering savings annually against budgets for ABC Plc.
- Initiated cost release programs for ZXY, saving 20% on direct costs.
- Initiated and facilitated a site-wide continuous improvement programme at XYZ, realising reduction of 15% of wasted product in Year 1.

Example 2: achievement bullet points for an information management specialist

- Designed and implemented a radically altered company-wide information management system for XYZX consolidating legal, safety, and operations information into a single system for multiple users.
- Created an indexed online system, reducing paper records for ABC by 75%.
- Refined a condensed information system for approx. 22,000 XYZ users.

- Managed a team of 12 data specialists at XYZ, anticipating and meeting training needs.
- Controlled budgets (of up to £110K p.a. at XYZ), for premises and archiving services.

About adjectives

Adjectives, if used too often, become an overdose of 'look at me'. They can easily tip into CV clichés. Phrases such as 'team player', 'self-starter', 'enthusiastic', or 'motivated' sound like you borrowed them from a CV guide. Some clichés are rescued by context; so, for example, 'team player' says virtually nothing, but 'the ideas person in the team' points to real situations. The real downside of clichés, apart from putting readers to sleep, is that stale phrases *make you sound like everyone else.* They make mature, experienced professionals sound like candidates just setting out on their careers. So your CV seems to say '*I have nothing to offer you can't get from a 21 year old*'. Not the best message.

Stripping back

Consider chopping out empty phrases such as 'hard-working', 'committed', and 'professional' – these qualities are expected in the workplace, but stating them suggests that they don't come naturally. Don't list personality traits – give examples demonstrating them. Use adjectives sparingly, and connect them to facts. In our survey, several HR managers stressed the need for documents that 'contain less self-praise and more objectivity around responsibilities and achievements' and demonstrate 'a passion for the area of work, crispness, no waffle, no overblown language'.

Try taking all the adjectives out of a line and seeing how it works. For example, you might begin with:

```
A dynamic, self-starting marketing professional with
drive and creative flair, experienced in managing
extensive budgets for above and below the line
activities on a range of exciting products.
```

Your first edit would therefore look like this:

```
A marketing professional with experience of managing
budgets for above and below the line activities on a
range of products.
```

Improved again as:

A marketing professional experienced as manager and budget holder for above and below the line promotion of homeware products.

Not perfect, but a good opening sentence for a profile.

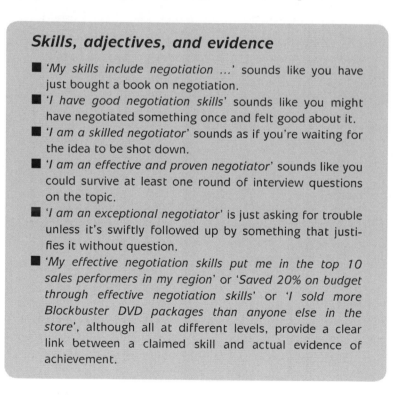

Skills, adjectives, and evidence

- *'My skills include negotiation ...'* sounds like you have just bought a book on negotiation.
- *'I have good negotiation skills'* sounds like you might have negotiated something once and felt good about it.
- *'I am a skilled negotiator'* sounds as if you're waiting for the idea to be shot down.
- *'I am an effective and proven negotiator'* sounds like you could survive at least one round of interview questions on the topic.
- *'I am an exceptional negotiator'* is just asking for trouble unless it's swiftly followed up by something that justifies it without question.
- *'My effective negotiation skills put me in the top 10 sales performers in my region'* or *'Saved 20% on budget through effective negotiation skills'* or *'I sold more Blockbuster DVD packages than anyone else in the store'*, although all at different levels, provide a clear link between a claimed skill and actual evidence of achievement.

How do I record achievements in a low-status job?

With routine jobs the problem isn't that people haven't done or achieved anything worth saying; the problem is identifying the things worth mentioning. Think carefully: most jobs provide some opportunity to learn, acquire skills, work with others, deal with customers (internal or external), organise and rethink working arrangements, meet targets, and acquire new responsibilities. The problem is usually not the job – people just don't ask enough questions about what they have done. So, instead of offering a throwaway line to sum up a fairly typical job:

```
Barista/waiter - Oddjobs Café               2005-2006
Range of general duties including bar and till work and
waiting on tables.
```

Try something much more likely to interest an employer:

Barista/waiter – Oddjobs Café   2005–2006
Learned a full range of barista and customer service skills in this city centre café serving Newtown's financial district.

- From zero experience, learned within three days how to serve the full range of hot beverages.
- Deputised for assistant manager during weekend shifts.
- Trained and supervised temp staff in the safe and efficient use of equipment.
- Mastered an electronic till.
- Contributed enthusiastically to the atmosphere of a lively and successful venue.

Achievements connected to soft skills

The final bullet point above is a 'soft' skill. Don't leave these out. They include influencing, persuading, supporting others, and communication. Many candidates find it hard to write about soft skills because these are not obviously linked to tangible outcomes. Yes, you may have won hearts and minds, but how do you record that?

Start by thinking about outcomes. How did your contribution make a difference? You might have won over an angry customer, helped a junior member of staff to learn the job, or communicated something tricky. At a more senior level you may have improved retention by helping someone's development, made teams work better, or persuaded people to change. If you can't quantify using numbers, tell the story of your results, for example, 'maintained team morale during a difficult takeover' or 'managed a number of difficult public meetings' or 'effectively protected my boss from internal pressures during a difficult press campaign'.

Key points from this chapter

✓ Dig deep in your evidence to find achievements – they turn the facts of your work history into memorable stories.

✓ Trim your text down: short phrases, short words.

✓ Focus on evidence of achievement rather than adjectives.

✓ Include evidence of soft skills – and their impact.

✓ Show rather than tell when communicating personality.

10

The art of profile writing

This chapter helps you to:

- Learn when and how to use a profile in your CV
- Understand how your profile provides a 'handover' to the reader
- Build your profile up step by step
- Avoid the classic errors and pitfalls of profile writing

> '*Think like a wise man but communicate in the language of the people.*' William Butler Yeats

Sink or swim – the CV profile

There are two important groups of people who will read your CV: people who make decisions, and people who influence decision-makers. Both groups are busy people who are probably only going to look in any detail at the first third of page 1 of your CV. If that doesn't get the main points across, you've lost their attention.

As discussed previously, if you were presenting your CV in person you'd probably say something like 'before you read this, let me tell you …'. What you're really saying is 'please notice this', 'don't look at that' and 'let me tell you the things I didn't mention'. Usually you won't be in the room when someone reads your CV, so it should tell its own story – without you looking over its shoulder.

A profile is your way of telling the reader what to notice, and how to see you. It's the hardest part of your CV to write, and, since it draws on your very best evidence, you probably can't compose it until the rest of your CV has taken shape.

You will see some CV guides telling you that the profile has had its day. It hasn't. In our survey, a majority of employers confirmed that well-written profiles are read with interest. One respondent approved of the 'greater effective use of achievement summaries at the beginning of CVs', and an HR manager praised 'better attempts to tailor really key information into the earlier part of the CV'. Profiles are welcomed if they are strongly connected to the job and give clear reasons why you should be interviewed.

Why the average profile bores, irritates, or fails to convince

Too many profiles are badly written – overstuffed with empty adjectives and clichés. In our survey, one HR specialist sent in a sample of the kind of profile she hates:

```
I am an outgoing, hard-working and self-motivated
individual who is used to people-facing roles and
can communicate and liaise with people both within
and outside all levels of an organisation. I have a
friendly and approachable manner and possess excellent
communication skills, which I believe makes me a real
team player.
```

A busy employer will become irritated by this offering for a number of reasons:

■ It's full of clichés such as 'self-motivated' and 'team player'. What do these phrases actually mean? Where's the evidence?
■ It tries to impress by claiming things that employers take for granted in good recruits such as working hard and communicating.

■ It makes sweeping statements that suggest perfection rather than strengths ('communicate and liaise with people both within and outside all levels of an organisation').

■ It makes strong claims, for example, 'excellent communication skills'. Excellent by whose standards?

■ It's entirely me-focused – 'I ... I ... I ...'. There is no reference to employer needs or problems.

■ It comes across as naive and immature.

One sentence at a time

A profile needs to be concise to be effective. Too much text provides a large block which readers tend to skip over, seeking out short bursts of information. If you can't get your messages across in a maximum of five lines, the profile is probably too complicated.

Structuring a CV profile: you/where/what/next

■ **You**: who you are in terms of occupational background and experience.

■ **Where**: your sector knowledge and experience of different kinds of organisations.

■ **What**: what do you have to offer in terms of know-how and skills, what have you done and achieved? What in your mix of skills and experience makes you unusual or attractive?

■ **Next**: what's next? What kind of role, organisation, culture and challenges would provide the right next step for you? (You won't always need this – see below.)

Here's an example of a Logistics Supervisor's profile at a rough first draft stage.

```
Richard Truckmaster

I am a committed and loyal staff member with an
excellent attendance record. I have worked my way
up from entry positions in a range of occupations,
and gained important experience in distribution and
logistics. I am now returning to the labour market
after retraining. I am looking for an opportunity to
prove myself as a hard-working and highly motivated
team player who will add value to your business.
```

Recruiters see a lot of profiles like this. 'I am' three times is repetitive, and writing a profile in the first person can make it sound like a begging letter. The profile is full of phrases that sound positive but are not linked to examples or evidence. More worrying, the profile draws attention to things that an employer almost takes for granted, for example, 'excellent attendance record' and 'hard-working'. It's almost as if this candidate wants to be thanked for doing the ordinary, basic parts of the job.

Part 1: you

Look again at the first sentence of Richard's profile: 'I am a committed and loyal staff member with an excellent attendance record.' It is the first full sentence of the CV, and is therefore the sentence which is read with the greatest attention. It is the paper equivalent of your first 30 seconds in the job interview: first impressions count. The danger is that a reader will take one glance at this list of adjectives and will ignore the rest of the profile.

Getting the **you** opening in the profile right requires you to think about **healthy pigeon-holing** (see Chapter 12, page 128). It's better to give a reader a handle to grab onto – a phrase which describes the kind of work you do. This might look like a kind of job title, even if it doesn't exactly match jobs you've held in the past. For example, 'qualified laboratory supervisor with extensive experience in the pharmaceutical sector' is clear, focused, and a good indication of role, responsibility and sector experience.

Link this information to clues about your academic background and professional status. Using the word 'graduate' in your profile (for example, 'graduate sales manager with 10 years' experience in the automotive sector') probably says as much as you want to say. A professional qualification or MBA can also be mentioned quickly and economically (for example, 'MBA-qualified communications office manager').

After some work Richard's *you* sentence was rewritten as follows:

> An MBA-qualified professional with 12 years' successful track record of
> managerial roles in transport and logistics.

This opening is brief but gets across primary messages (background, track record, work sectors, supporting qualifications). Most importantly it defines in (relatively) tight terms the role he wants to fill, and its seniority.

Some further *you* sentence examples which clearly set out each candidate's main work focus:

> A qualified book-keeper with a strong track record of credit control.

> An accomplished Executive PA with experience of supporting Board Level
> Directors in a range of blue-chip organisations.

> A 3D Design graduate specialising in building 4-metre high puppets for street
> theatre events.

The *you* sentence may need to be an overview of your career, *looked at from the perspective of your most recent successes*. So a sentence that begins '*Starting with a degree in Business Studies, and after setting up my own business as a freelance photographer, I have most recently become an HR specialist*' fails, by offering the reader far too many distractions along the way. A better, simpler approach might read:

> A graduate HR professional with extensive experience of talent retention.

Part 2: where?

If it helps to say you've worked extensively in one sector, or a variety of sectors, get that point across here. Sentence 2 (it could of course also be the second half of sentence 1) will often provide a swift overview of the sectors you have worked in, and the kind of organisations you know well.

In this case, Richard's draft profile is going to state simply: 'Experience includes print trade and hospitality.' Other example *where?* statements include:

> With extensive experience in motor manufacturing and design ...

> With a background in customer service improvement across a range of sectors ...

> Experience in the hotel, catering, leisure and corporate events sectors.

Part 3: what?

The *what?* section in your profile may take one or two sentences to communicate. Here's the meat in the sandwich: your work experience and main skills. Your main focus should be on shouting out 'achievement' rather than 'potential'. If you're relatively new to the labour market don't let this put you off (see Chapter 9 on achievements).

Richard's original profile stated: *'I have worked my way up from entry positions in a range of occupations, and gained important experience in distribution and logistics. I am now returning to the labour market after retraining.'* These two sentences avoid making claims, apart from the weak 'important experience'. They also introduce negative thoughts – a 'range' of occupations? Does he find it difficult to stick to one career path? Why did he need to leave the labour market and get retrained?

Richard's revised *What?* section:

> An experienced leader with expertise in leading and motivating teams working under pressure.

Part 4: next

In a few short sentences you've established who you are and what you have done. The last might be about what's **next** in your career, clearly suggesting that you have a plan. You might want to use a **next** sentence if you want to make a career change. You've set out your background and your skill set, so it makes sense to say what you want next.

Richard's present offering is: '*I am looking for an opportunity to prove myself as a hard-working and highly motivated team player who will add value to your business.*' This just doesn't cut the mustard. It strays into empty claims and starts to sound like a begging letter.

Some career coaches recommend putting in a career objective or 'target job', for example, '*currently seeking a role as a Marketing Director in the FMCG sector*'. If you really have just one job in your sights, this might work, but you have to find words *that are meaningful to each and every potential employer.*

Do not use a **next** sentence if you are applying for a specific job. Putting in the exact title of the job you're applying for sounds cheesy – and including a target job that is a poor match for the role on offer means you're sunk. See below for Richard's revised **next** statement.

Combined effect: the completed profile

Here's the revised profile which captures the most important things about Richard in four sentences. It mixes *claims* and *evidence*, and now includes a (not too prescriptive) target role. It is in the **smart third person** (see Chapter 8, page 84). The profile may need more work, but it's good enough to market test:

> An MBA-qualified professional with 12 years' successful track record of managerial roles in transport and logistics. Experience includes print trade and

hospitality. An experienced leader with expertise in leading and motivating teams working under pressure. Currently seeking a decision-making role in a forward-looking organisation with a focus on continual performance improvement.

Other example profiles

Different examples of profiles are set out below, along with comments about why they might succeed or fail.

Profile A: vague

```
A talented, dynamic performer, I am a good communicator
in speech and writing, with a mix of analytical and
creative thinking. Highly motivated and a strong team
player, I am seeking the next big challenge … .
```

These flowery adjectives set off all kinds of alarm bells and push the reader into a hostile position. This approach fails because it makes no mention of jobs, organisations, or work sectors. It makes sweeping claims, but where's the evidence? An interviewer is going to have a field day probing the lack of facts and demolishing your claims so fast that the only thing on your CV you're prepared to defend is your name and address.

Our survey confirms the fact that employers dislike 'people overselling themselves in their CVs'. Another respondent complained about the mismatch between profile and reality: 'Personally, I do not like the personal profile paragraph unless it says something specific. Naturally, only positives are going to be highlighted, but too many profiles say that the individual is a good communicator, etc., but this is often not backed up at interview.'

Profile B: a graduate overselling limited experience

A creative, clear thinking graduate with wide-ranging experience gained in a number of media-related temporary positions. An experienced communicator with excellent written and verbal skills and wide-ranging experience of working in many different environments. I am focused and determined, and have excellent powers of persuasion. My previous posts have required me to be flexible, to use my own initiative, work well in a team, have a sense of humour and to be able to prioritise workloads. I am very well organised in my methods of working and enjoy paying attention to detail.

In all fairness, it's tough writing a profile if you're new to the marketplace. Very typically, this offering lists qualities not skills. It translates as 'I have very little experience, but some potential'. The first sentence feels like an apology – 'I haven't had a proper job in the media'. This profile also takes a scattergun approach, trying to appeal to as wide an audience as possible. This candidate's career coach got back to basics: 'what have you actually *done*? (in your studies, in your temporary work, on work experience, anywhere?)'. The revised version is set out below (and may need to be followed by some useful bullet points using the profile plus method – see Chapter 11, pages 119–21).

Redrafted profile B

A graduate communications specialist with experience in the leisure management, communication, and PR sectors. Proven written communications skills, excellent powers of persuasion and public speaking ability to business audiences, accompanied by a track record of clear thinking, problem solving, and getting teams to achieve results on target. Now seeking a role requiring the ability to anticipate consumer demands and deliver effective solutions.

Profile C: business analyst profile, adjective heavy

A successful, experienced and focused IT business
analyst with a background in financial applications
within an SAP environment. Talented at managing
teams, with well-developed negotiation skills and
recent exposure to a large-scale company integration.
A professional, results-oriented graduate with an
excellent academic record and a track record of
success, well respected by colleagues and managers
alike. A hard-working and committed individual who
strives to deliver a quality result for the business
and its customers.

This is halfway there, but has too many adjectives. Its 74 words include the following: *successful/experienced/focused/ talented with well-developed negotiation skills/professional/ results-oriented/graduate with an excellent academic record/track record of success/well respected/hard-working/committed/strives to deliver.* All high-blown claims, with barely a single piece of evidence in sight. A reworked version of the IT business analyst profile might read as below.

Redrafted profile C

A highly experienced graduate business analyst with good working knowledge
of a range of financial applications and a track record of success in SAP
environments. Well-developed leadership, negotiation, and change management
skills. Now seeking a challenging role in an organisation determined to achieve
quality results and the highest levels of customer satisfaction.

Profile D: IT Specialist, full of techno jargon

Highly experienced graduate working as IS Development
Manager with skills across broad ranges of hardware and
software systems. Experienced in IBM AS/400, IBM System
34/36/38, MS Project, RPG III & IV. Skilled within
international, multi-site, multi-company structures.
Uniquely combines an eye for detail with a flair for
developing creative solutions, to facilitate the

```
co-ordination of important, complex and high-value
projects.
```

This profile is a good example of the limiting effect of the opening statement. If you tell the reader you're a computing graduate in a computing job, you can't really be surprised that you're not invited for general management roles. The technology is of course out of date. However, it's clear from the final sentence that this candidate wants to break out of the box and move into a more general project management role. If so, the jargon is off-putting. A better profile translates IT experience into the language of business solutions, and brings out more transferable skills.

Redrafted profile D

Accomplished graduate systems development manager with broad experience of international, multi-site, and multi-company structures. Strong technical background combined with effective people skills and a flair for developing creative solutions. Seeking a role managing creative projects from concept to implementation.

Key points from this chapter

✓ Only write the profile when you have completed every other part of the CV.
✓ Construct it one sentence at a time using **you/where/ what/next**.
✓ Avoid excessive use of adjectives and too much focus on personal characteristics.
✓ Give maximum attention to the opening sentence – it may open doors or close them immediately.

Getting more out of your profile

This chapter helps you to:

■ Smarten up your profile layout
■ Adopt the profile plus model to integrate achievement bullet points into your profile
■ Consider using a reference quote instead of, or alongside, your profile
■ Build on your profile to improve your networking messages

> *'It requires a very unusual mind to undertake the analysis of the obvious.'* Alfred N. Whitehead

Getting the profile layout right

When you've got the wording right, pay attention to layout. So, for example, here's the layout of the profile in a CV for a recent graduate:

Ned Student

Location: Hightown |t: 02480 567899 | m: 06777 654321 | e: nstudent@example.com
LI: uk.linkedin.com/NedStudent1

A design graduate with developed customer service skills acquired from a range of contexts including hospitality, tourism, market research, sales and promotions, archiving, and previous volunteer experience working in a specialist wildlife centre.

As with other CV examples in this book, the profile comes straight after the contact details. It is printed bold, left-justified rather than centred, and relatively short. This is one occasion where bold print really grabs attention. There's no need to title it 'Profile' – it's clear what it is. Here are further examples of fairly effective profiles laid out the same way:

Experienced retail assistant with a record of achieving increases in sales turnover and customer loyalty in healthcare products.

European Sales Manager with excellent influencing skills plus 12 years' experience in successfully building and leading sales operations for major European corporations. Multi-lingual (native French speaker, business standard English and German). Demonstrable results in working across varying cultures, building key accounts, and making a significant contribution to organisational efficiency, growth and profitability. Seeking a challenging opportunity to develop sales management of high-quality, luxury brands across European markets.

Profile plus

Research reveals that employers find it helpful to see tangible evidence summarised. One HR manager welcomed CVs containing 'more focus on achievements rather than duties alone'. Another HR director wrote: 'It is helpful that applicants point out strengths and achievements rather than leaving you trawling through everything and having to draw your own conclusions about what they may have achieved in a particular role.' How are you going to choose the best information?

Fans of the profile-led CV used to recommend having a section titled 'Key skills and achievements' or 'Key achievements'. Such information shouldn't need a heading because the material should speak for itself. Also, market feedback suggests that readers have become irritated by a long, disconnected list of achievements because:

- Examples may come from way back in the candidate's history.
- It's difficult to see which roles achievements apply to.
- The term 'key skills' is widely used for secondary school students, so is inappropriate for the workplace.

The mix & match CV format allows you to showcase a short number of your very best bullet points. This can be very useful (a) if your best evidence isn't in your most recent job and you want to highlight it on page 1, or (b) if you want to make a career change and your most recent job evidence pushes you in the wrong direction.

Using a **profile plus** allows you to sneak just a little more information into the top part of page 1 and show off your best material. Try adding some bullet points to your profile. There's a wrong way of doing it, as the following draft shows:

```
A graduate sales professional with B2B experience
focused on the information security needs of the
insurance sector and a track record of achievement in
building customer awareness.

■ Professional approach
■ Familiar with Microsoft Office
■ Methodical and reliable
■ Capable of working in a team or on my own.
```

Here the opening profile works well but the following bullet points are weak, don't add anything, and undermine the strength of the first statement. Revised, the bullet points not only connect (see the use of the colon at the end of the profile) but add strong, immediate pieces of evidence:

A graduate sales professional with B2B experience focused on the information security needs of the insurance sector and a track record of achievement in building customer awareness:

- Redesigned sales manual.
- Experience of providing technical support to business users.
- Introduced improved web-based record keeping systems.
- Achieved a work experience placement at XYZ Insurance in the face of strong competition.

The **profile plus** therefore once again breaks the rules of CV composition in order to highlight a shortlist of achievements on page 1. In addition to a profile, you include three or four relevant, strong bullet points, without any title. So for a more senior candidate:

> A business development specialist with a strong track record in developing brands and organisations. Accomplished across a wide range of sectors including FMCG. Proven creative expertise in brand development, sales, customer service and driving growth through marketing initiatives and the rapid exploitation of new markets.
>
> ■ Managed website launch for ABC Finance driving a £2.8 billion business.
> ■ Repositioned No Debt Brand for XYZ arriving at a 40% increase in sales.
> ■ Doubled sales of Acme Pay to £8m in 15 months.
> ■ Increased NiceBank home loans sales from £20m to £70m.

The profile plus method is to be used with care. Essentially you're deciding on three or four exceptionally strong pieces of evidence to reveal very early on when you've got maximum reader interest. If this information can be fitted into a short profile you won't need additional bullet points. Similarly, if this evidence jumps off the page from your most recent job, a simple profile will be enough.

Quoting a reference

A number of CVs in the market right now quote from a reference, a letter of recommendation, or a supportive statement from a LinkedIn connection. This comes instead of (or after) your profile.

The jury's out on whether this will become a trend, but the approach seems acceptable to employers. Quoting a reference like this appeals to those who feel that their own words in a profile are a sales pitch. Only use a reference if it's from someone senior enough to matter, and only if it contains evidence rather than simply saying how wonderful you are. Include the date after the quote to show that it is recent. You might use the quote on its own or combine it with a profile as below:

A qualified information specialist with scientific and technical experience, with a track record of analysing, organising and implementing effective information solutions. Familiar with a wide range of IT solutions. Expertise in environmental and legacy issues:

'Jane is an expert in locating, managing and interpreting complex environmental research who would be an asset to any business dealing with environmental litigation'. John Smith, General Counsel – 2012.

Using your profile as part of your networking

Imagine you're at a social event and you mention that you're job hunting. You're asked, 'what are you looking for?'. Some candidates waste the opportunity talking about the difficulties of the job market; others about their uncertain career direction. Some just mention a job title. The problem with job titles is that they mean different things in different organisations. Besides, few people have access to vacancies, and you're not yet known well enough to get recommended.

Try saying something different. What works best is a short summary of your main work focus, your background, your primary skills, and the kind of role you're looking for. This is sometimes described as the 'elevator pitch' – what you would say to an interviewer who meets you in reception and, taking you up in the lift, says 'tell me about yourself' between floors. Your CV profile provides the key ingredients. You don't have to get every element across – two or three ingredients are enough to capture attention and stick in someone's memory. That's how people get remembered and become visible in the hidden job market.

To shorten your job search time, get a short burst of important information across every time you're asked what you're looking for. You don't have to over-sell, just indicate the right ingredients for a future role, getting your ideal job recipe across in a quick, uncomplicated way, for example, 'I'm an information specialist with extensive knowledge of the legal sector. I'm looking for a role where I can help an organisation manage and source the most up-to-date business information.' You can do this in a verbal statement (to employers, recruitment consultants and networking contacts). You can also adopt a more economical style for emails – rather than send your CV, send bullet points based on **you/where/what/ next**.

Key points from this chapter

✓ Refine, edit, and test your profile.
✓ Pay careful attention to layout.
✓ Add bullet points using the profile plus model if that helps you foreground vital details.
✓ Consider whether quoting from a reference will work.
✓ Use compressed messages in every aspect of your job search – particularly networking.

12

Fine tuning page 1

This chapter helps you to:

- See page 1 as a single-page advertisement
- Seek healthy pigeon-holing
- Decide where to position information about your learning and qualifications
- Use the 'so what?' test
- Spot the dangers of trying to communicate personality

> *'Short words are the best and old words when short are best of all.'*   Winston Churchill

Opening shot

Having gathered evidence, captured your past work perform-ance, and listed your strongest skills and achievements, it's time to finalise page 1.

Print off page 1 of your CV. Now tear off the top third of this sheet. Look at what it says and how much information is actually helpful to you. Imagine that someone was walking round at a conference promoting you on the basis of this slip of paper. Or someone's computer screen has frozen and won't scroll down any further than this point. What would this first 33% of page 1 say about you? Would it capture the main things you want people to be saying about you?

Here is some advice that is worth the cover price of this book on its own:

The first page is the page that matters
and
the first half page matters most.

Your CV will be read quickly. The whole document may be read in under five minutes, but this will only happen if you grab the reader's attention in the first 20 seconds or so. The first question a reader asks is *'is this CV worth my time?'* – a question answered in the kind of time you spend glancing at a web page. To get someone to keep reading, a CV has to answer the question *'does this person have anything we want?'*. The average reader decides whether to read on with attention about halfway down page 1. Only after holding someone's interest for a few minutes are you likely to prompt the question *'should we get this person in for interview?'*. (See also Chapter 14, pages 154–5, on how recruitment consultancies react to page 1 of your CV.)

The target length for your CV is two pages (see Chapter 13, page 136). You might get away with three pages if your history requires it – but only if page 1 works. Page 1 forces a reader to decide whether to read any further. Page 1 is your advertising billboard, your shop window, and the opening part of this page matters more than anything else, because that's where the important decisions are made. Say the things that matter early on, while you've got the reader's attention, and don't include non-vital information on page 1.

Messages sent out by your name and address

If the opening half of your CV has the biggest impact, what can go right or wrong when you do the most basic thing – set out your contact details? Here's one example:

```
May Elizabeth Jean Example BA (Hons), MA, MCIPD,
                    Cert RP
                   Flat 1B
               12 The High Street
              Little High Village
                  Hightown
                  Highshire
                   HH1 S99
   (but currently at Flat 9, Longtown, Longwayoff, LL1 L99
                 until 1 April)
   t: 09234 567890 or 03351 12345 (please leave a message)
                 m: 77890 12345
           email: xrdgdred12432@complexity.com
```

The example above takes 10 lines of valuable CV space, and includes all kinds of irrelevant and distracting detail. Keep it simple and uncluttered:

Jean Example
Location: Hightown | m: 77890 12345 | e: jexample@example.com
LI: uk.linkedin.com/JeanExample

Note the vertical line between each part of the address line (to find this on most keyboards, hold down shift and press the backslash key). This design feature may not appeal to you, but current feedback suggests that most readers find this design effect helpful. It's useful because it allows you to fit several separate pieces of information on one line.

Put your name in bold, in a slightly bigger font (try Calibra 14pt), right at the top of the document. That's the title of your document; it's the equivalent of your personal logo. Include your name as you would use it if answering the phone at work. So if your name is Christopher John Smith but everyone calls you John, print 'John Smith'.

Include the town you live in rather than the full postal address. If you live in a small village identify the broad area, for example, 'West Yorkshire' and if you live in a big city identify a district or postal area (for example, 'SE3' or 'Lewisham'). Consider the impact of this location carefully. If you're seeking a senior role it's likely that applications will come from a wide area, but if the role is less senior and unlikely to attract a relocation package your location may put an employer off (here a covering letter may help to explain why the target location is attractive or convenient to you – you might, for example, be about to move house).

Keep your contact details up to date. Include just one email address – not alternatives – and check it at least twice a day. If you mainly use your mobile, just give that number, but make sure it's set up for voicemail – it's amazing how many job seekers have a mobile number that rings out if not answered. Check voicemail frequently so you can return phone calls the same day.

Where should qualifications be mentioned?

As Chapter 7 outlined, it's your choice whether you detail your qualifications on page 1. Unless your qualifications and study history are *directly* related to the job, put them on page 2.

You may be able to explain their relevance. One of my clients was a sharp, business-focused accountant with a degree in Classics. He made play of the fact that his knowledge of the Roman Empire gave him a great grounding for the cut and thrust of organisational change.

You might turn your learning history into an achievement, for example, 'Achieved MA in HRD while holding down a full-time role'. Alternatively you might sum up your learning history in one or two words in the profile (for example, 'graduate' or 'professionally qualified'). Some organisations are looking for particular technical or professional qualifications (for example, in health and safety or accountancy or an MBA). If so, state that qualification loud and clear on page 1 in the profile or just below it.

The first 15 words

It's amazing how often CV problems are diagnosed or solved by attention to the opening 15 words. For some candidates those words will be wasted saying 'full clean driving licence' or, if there's a profile, 'Enthusiastic, reliable, self-starting …'.

The way you describe yourself in the opening sentence of your profile does a huge amount of work – or damage. It sets the tone, and also plants information in the reader's mind. If your first words are vague, your application is seen as vague. If you use too many adjectives, you're seen as boastful and disconnected from the reality of the job. If you make claims without evidence, you're seen as someone unlikely to deliver.

Any information you provide in the first 15 words or so makes a big impact, so think carefully what you place there, whether it's your degree subject or your last job title.

Healthy pigeon-holing: managing the way you are labelled

Being put in the wrong pigeon-hole happens all the time. Perhaps you're always being asked to serve on committees, and hate doing so. Perhaps you're always called on as the 'IT person' simply because you once set up a new PC.

No one likes being labelled with a job title they're uncomfortable with. It's even worse to be a square peg pushed into a round hole simply because agencies and your network always see you in terms of your last job. If you're trying to make a career change, being associated with the wrong kind of job frustrates progress. However, much of this labelling is something you do to yourself. For example, many people who want to break out of accountancy have a CV and LinkedIn profile which begins '*A qualified accountant who* ...'. However, the initial labelling we do when we glance at a CV can also work in your favour by setting out your career aim.

Read your profile again. Highlight the words that are already putting you into boxes you don't want to occupy. Your opening sentence probably labels you. For example, writing '*A Modern Languages graduate who* ...' suggests you're looking for a job using a foreign language. Early mentions of any specialism can do two things: label you very effectively, or narrow your options far too soon.

Healthy pigeon-holing starts to work in your favour once you find words to describe your past in the language of the work you'd like to find. So our accountant might begin '*A business-focused project manager who* ...', and our Modern Languages graduate '*A customer experience specialist with a background in* ...'. Your first 15 words will often dictate what you get offered – particularly those who skim-read your CV to match you to job titles, such as recruitment consultants.

Big ticket items

The strongest CV material is most closely related to the job you're chasing. There are also other high value, 'big ticket' items that experienced recruiters and careers specialists know will help your CV to get noticed:

■ A relevant role mentioned in your profile (see healthy pigeon-holing above).

- Relevant job titles in your work history.
- Names of large, well-known organisations.
- Direct language focusing on outcomes rather than attempts to describe your personal qualities.
- Achievements which an employer would like you to repeat.
- Quantified results.
- Skills identified in the kind of language an employer uses to describe top performers.
- Action words indicating candidates who take the initiative and achieve results.
- A coherent career 'story' which makes sense and suggests you have consciously made decisions which have moved you forward.

First page errors

Based on feedback to our CV research, here's what typically goes wrong with the first page of a CV:

- Upside down: the CV starts with non-essential information, and hides the good stuff on pages 2 or 3.
- No clear message: your CV fails to get its main points across.
- Profile crash: your initial summary confuses, irritates, and sends out all the wrong messages or no message at all.
- Over-egged: your first page oversells you dreadfully.
- Overload: trying to make too many points. Too many bullet points in your profile plus section (see Chapter 11, pages 119–21) will persuade the reader to skip them.
- Contradictory: the reader gets multiple, conflicting pictures.
- Jumble sale: it's full of disconnected information.
- Wastes time on the obvious: your CV offers no additional insights beyond what the general reader could guess from your list of job titles.

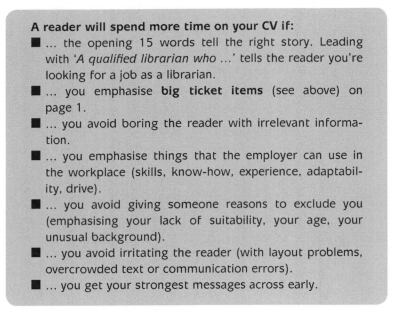

A reader will spend more time on your CV if:

■ ... the opening 15 words tell the right story. Leading with '*A qualified librarian who ...*' tells the reader you're looking for a job as a librarian.

■ ... you emphasise **big ticket items** (see above) on page 1.

■ ... you avoid boring the reader with irrelevant information.

■ ... you emphasise things that the employer can use in the workplace (skills, know-how, experience, adaptability, drive).

■ ... you avoid giving someone reasons to exclude you (emphasising your lack of suitability, your age, your unusual background).

■ ... you avoid irritating the reader (with layout problems, overcrowded text or communication errors).

■ ... you get your strongest messages across early.

The 'so what?' test

Too many of the draft profiles presented in Chapter 10 fail the easiest, most important, test you can apply to a draft CV, line by line – '**so what?**'. Wherever you mention a responsibility, a skill, an achievement, ask the same question: so what?. In CVs for relatively senior people I often find phrases like '*Responsible for staff training*' or '*Responsible for recruitment and selection*' or '*Undertook annual appraisals of staff*'. So what? Any candidate with a history of formal management will have done these things. Mentioning them makes the document sound like a CV for a far less experienced person. Equally, a phrase like '*IT competent*' may fail the same test – better to point to a real familiarity with computer applications.

If you find material in your CV that would be true of more junior candidates, rephrase or cut it out. The exception would be experience or qualifications you just have to mention to get shortlisted.

Content which works well on page 1

Your plan is to gain maximum control over the first page. The mix & match CV provides several blocks of information at your disposal (see Chapter 7). If you want to steer the reader in a particular direction you will probably use a **profile plus** to include bullet points drawing attention to tangible achievements (see Chapter 11, page 119). After that, you have some flexibility about what you include on page 1, but you should include detailed information on your most recent job at the bottom of the page.

The following example uses a clear layout on page 1 which uses bullet points after the profile and in the body of the CV:

Sara Workhard

The Brown House, Brown Street, Brownton, BN9 12F
t: 01234 567899 | m: 07777 654321 | e: sworkhard@example.com

An accomplished events management professional, qualified to Diploma level in Travel & Tourism, with a background of customer service experience in the events, hospitality, travel, and recruitment sectors. A track record as an effective organiser of resources and people with the ability to win commitment from individuals and organisations:
- Organised the largest charity dinner in the North East region in 2012.
- Sold exhibition space for two major regional events, ahead of time and target.
- Renegotiated all contracts with catering, AV, and printing suppliers saving 15% against budget.
- Increased click-through traffic to an events management website by 200% using a Twitter campaign.
- Instigated a new customer satisfaction improvement measure for Brownton Hotel.

QUALIFICATIONS & CONTINUING PROFESSIONAL DEVELOPMENT

BTEC National Diploma in Travel and Tourism, Brownton College, 2007.
Completed at Distinction level in every module. Modules included: Marketing; Business of Travel and Tourism; Retail Travel Operations; Customer Service; Tourism Development; Incoming Domestic Tourism; Business Travel; Special Interest Tourism; Hospitality and Conferences; and Exhibitions and Events.

Eight GCSEs at Grade C and above including English, Maths, Science (double award) and Spanish.

EMPLOYMENT HISTORY

Events Coordinator, Acme Events Ltd   Sept 2011 – June 2013
Supervised a team of staff and volunteers in this busy event management business.
- Liaised closely with corporate clients to maximise their budgets and event impact.
- Planned and launched a fundraising dinner for 300 in the North East region, co-ordinating all aspects before and during events with suppliers and staff.
- Drove sales of exhibition space for large consumer shows.
- Marketing – researched, planned and implemented marketing activities for the business.
- Researched and analysed customer feedback and footfall traffic to maximise the impact for future events.

Conference & Events Co-ordinator, Brownton Hotel and Spa   Mar 2009 – Sept 2011
Sole responsibility for all conference and events bookings and planning for a successful 5-star hotel.
- Selected as Employee of the Year 2011.
- Effective Communication – responded to enquiries, communicated options to the customer to achieve the best result.
- Event Co-ordination – worked closely with customers from enquiry to event completion – requiring product knowledge and meticulous attention to detail.
- Sales – met the Hotel's sales targets for weddings and conferences through telephone sales and face-to-face appointments. Hotel achieved the most improved conversion percentage within the group.
- Problem Solving – overcame a range of difficulties and logistical issues to meet customer needs.

Can you communicate personality?

Many candidates are eager to get their personality across on paper. This is harder than it looks. It's better to *show* rather than *tell* – use a strong example of being self-motivated rather than simply stating how you see yourself, which leads to problems of tone. If you feel the need to get your personality across on paper, consider this. You'll probably get it wrong. It's safer to rely on action verbs and listed achievements to give a clear indication of your working style.

However, be careful you don't strip your CV of personality entirely by describing only a narrow range of skills. If you list only 'dry', technical skills, you may miss out. An employer looking at two technical specialists may take the one who is also capable of explaining things to work colleagues. If you possess mainly technical skills, don't miss the opportunity to say something about supporting 'soft' interpersonal skills.

Attempts to communicate a quirky personality can get you into hot water. Writing '*my approach is a bit off the wall*' reads badly, and on paper the phrase '*people say I'm a bit of a character*' will set off alarm bells. However you'll probably still get away with '*thinks outside the box*', even though it's a cliché. Avoid claiming oddness in the interests section, too. If you're determined to mention your 37 unpublished novels, your lifelong passion for growing orchids, or your new-found allegiance to a political cause, your CV is not the right place to say so *unless it makes sense to the job*. Even a statement of personal faith on a CV often leads to the assumption that you hold hard-line views that will upset work colleagues. Readers interpret things in very one-dimensional terms.

Avoid apologising in a CV: describing your jobs as a 'miscellany' or 'unusual mix' is enough to convince the reader that you have no idea where your career is heading. Find a style and tone that match your seniority. Use a business-like tone throughout.

Key points from this chapter

✓ Grasp the power of page 1 material, and how you can get it wrong.
✓ Manage the process of healthy pigeon-holing.
✓ Understand the impact of the first 15 words.
✓ Focus on big ticket items.
✓ Apply the **so what?** test to your draft.
✓ Look at the positives and negatives in your CV that will be drawn out at interview.

13

FAQs and checklists
for your final edit

This chapter helps you to:

- Pose frequently asked questions about CV writing
- Deal with tricky issues such as redundancy
- Check style, layout, and tone
- Follow a practical checklist for your final edit

'Reality is frequently inaccurate.' Douglas Adams

How long should my CV be?

Over-long CVs indicate a lack of focus and an insecurity verging on desperation. Ideally your CV should not be longer than two pages, and page 1 is the page that matters. If however you have a valid reason for running over to three pages, it's not a disaster – better than cramming everything in and losing valuable white space.

Be guided by what is considered the norm in your sector. A marketing CV will rarely be more than two pages, while an academic CV may go over three pages if it includes a long list of publications. Career coach Ruth Winden advises: 'Go through your CV and cut, cut, cut. Be ruthless. Every word has to be relevant and earn its place.'

Submitting your CV electronically

Careers specialist Zena Everett provides a useful reminder: 'When you submit a CV electronically just title the file with your name, not "JohnadminCV2013" or anything which might give the impression that you have lots of options and have been on the market for some time.'

What about email addresses?

A CV without an email address is asking for trouble – it broadcasts the fact that you don't know or don't care about modern technology. Make sure the email address is not so complex that it is difficult to copy, and business-like (for example, 'bev.smith@example.com' rather than 'bevsmiffy' or 'madbevvy' or 'housewifey' or any of the other endearing addresses we love to use with our friends. Recruiter Graeme Dixon, Director of the Oportunis Group, reminds you: 'Look at the email address you use to send the CV. I have seen everything, including sexy101xxx@ and bigmonster@. And if you are sending it via email do you need a postal address?'

What's the best way to present my contact details?

Although this seems a very obvious point, double check each digit of your telephone numbers and each character of your email address. A recruiter will only make one attempt to reach you. Print your name in the exact form you want it to be used in interview. Otherwise you begin your document by misdirecting your reader. If your name is Alexander Benjamin Smith but everyone calls you Ben, then simply put 'Ben

Smith' in large letters across the top of the CV (see Chapter 12, page 126).

Set up voicemail and check it at least twice a day. Do the same with your email inbox. Failure to respond quickly to a message from a recruiter or employer is usually taken as lack of interest. If it's easier to just give out a mobile number, that's fine.

Should I include a target job statement?

There are some circumstances when you might include a 'target job' statement on a CV. At one stage recruiters encouraged candidates to put this boldly at the header of a CV, for example, 'Target Job – Retail Manager'. This is rarely a good idea, although if your CV is aimed at exploring the market you might make a broad statement about the kind of role you're after (not one job) in the last line of your profile (see Chapter 10, page 113). Kate Howlett writes: 'Don't mention a target job if the CV is sent in response to a specific vacancy. Your ideal next job should seem to be the job on offer.'

How far back should I go when listing jobs?

In general, most employers only want to focus in detail on your last five years, and probably want only outline detail of jobs you did over 10 years ago. The main rule here is clarity of message. If you did a very important job 18 years ago that shaped your whole CV, you need to mention it. However, if your past contains few surprises it's probably not important to list every role you've undertaken since you left full-time education. Doing so often gives unnecessary emphasis to your age, but don't make the mistake of leaving them out – recruitment consultants in particular get rather concerned about gaps in your CV. With jobs you did some time back it's often fine to put them in blocks (for example, 'Various secretarial/PA roles, 1992–1997' or 'Engineering Apprenticeship, followed by a range of positions as Electronic Engineer, 1988–1992'. If an employer wants more details you can provide them on request.

Should I include reasons for job change?

There is no requirement to give reasons for job change in your CV itself, and volunteering your reasons on paper usually means asking for trouble. However, do be prepared to deal with this issue at interview. If you were dismissed from a role at any stage in the past you may be legally required to state this on an application form or if asked a direct question at interview. If you changed jobs because you couldn't stand your boss or hated the organisation then keep it to yourself – that information should never go anywhere near a recruiter.

Should I mention the fact I was made redundant?

Similarly, there is no reason to mention redundancy on a CV. Remember that a large proportion of the workforce have experienced redundancy, and it is not a statement that you failed or under-performed. At interview deal with the topic by quickly moving the conversation on to the future: *'As you know, XYZ went through a restructuring process, and like many people I was laid off this year. This has given me a good opportunity to rethink my career options and I am now very focused on the kind of job that would really suit me ...'*

Should I mention my current or last salary?

Some CV readers say they find it useful to know what you've been earning as a rough guide to whether the role is right for you. However, including your salary details on a CV can lead to problems. It may rule you out where an employer has in mind a significantly lower salary than you have received. Equally, if the prospective salary is a lot more than you are currently receiving, your current pay level may be taken as an indicator of your ability. On balance, it's best to keep salary information off your CV, particularly as the document may be circulated widely. Answer the question verbally or in a cover letter.

Definitely don't put any information in your CV about the salary you are seeking. That's a matter for interview strategy (covered in depth in my book *Job Interviews: Top Answers To Tough Questions*).

My work experience is a jumble sale – what do I do?

This is where a lot of people begin. Their qualifications don't relate to their work history, their most recent job is a distraction, and taken together the listed jobs seem to have no relationship with each other.

The problem is that if you haven't made sense of your work history, no one else will. Remember that people change jobs much more frequently than they used to and it's now far more acceptable to demonstrate variety and unusual backgrounds in your CV. If you are going to make your history seem like it has a sense of direction, you will almost certainly need to use a profile to tie it all together. Try to see a pattern; for example, you may discover that all of your jobs have been about motivating people or solving problems or providing excellent customer service.

How do I deal with complex job titles and job functions?

Think about the likely reader. Explain unusual roles or titles in plain English, and briefly. Too many CVs lose their way because they use undigested jargon or get into overcomplicated terminology. Learn how to write simple straightforward English, for example, 'Customer Service Advisor – provided speedy, efficient and friendly response to consumer complaints by telephone and letter'.

What about overseas jobs?

There is no reason why you shouldn't gain brownie points in your CV by writing about work in other countries. It can provide supporting evidence of cross-cultural experience, language skills, or breadth of experience. Do ensure that you make it clear that you are looking for a UK role, or an employer may assume that you'd rather pursue an international career. And do translate foreign job titles or terminology into user-friendly English.

Do I have to mention exact dates of employment?

Following the introduction of age discrimination laws in the UK, confusion reigns about whether you should include dates in a CV. You are not required to include dates of any kind in a CV. However, you run the risk of your CV being excluded if you do not include the start and end dates for each job. Our CV survey shows that 97% of employers still want to see information about the dates you were employed. Keep a record of your exact employment dates in your **CV data bank** (Chapter 4, page 38) for reference.

Sixty per cent of employers surveyed want to know the date you became qualified. Listing the study institution, dates, and your final grade adds credibility. Some employers will wish to check your work history, and may want to see original copies of certificates and qualifications.

You are, however, *not* required to include your age or date of birth on your CV, and it's not a good idea to include either. Other CV content may, of course, give this information away, for example the date you graduated or completed an apprenticeship.

How do I deal with gaps in my CV?

There is no point trying to hide gaps in your work history. It's one of the first things a recruiter looks for. Make sure you cover each relevant period of your work history. If you don't, a recruiter may assume all the wrong things, such as a long and difficult job-search period or lack of focus and direction. Here are some of the main reasons why you might have CV gaps, and some ways of dealing with them:

1 **Job-searching.** Write positively about your job search, and any work you have done, including unpaid work, for example, *'kept my skills up to date on voluntary assignments and enjoyed the opportunity of investigating a wide range of organisations'*.
2 **Undertaking temporary work.** Consider each temporary job as work experience providing skills and sector knowledge. Write briefly about each role and how it has added to your employability.

3 **Study.** If it was study around a subject that is not strictly related to your career, spell out the transferable skills acquired.

4 **Travel or other career break.** A great opportunity to write about what you did, what you learned and how you did it. Negotiating a career break and doing something interesting may be what makes you distinctive.

5 **Family commitments.** You may have had to take time out because of family responsibilities. Here again, be absolutely straight about what you did (possibly referring to what you learned in the process) rather than leaving a blank.

6 **Other difficulties.** Take advice about what you have to say legally. Then convey a simple message: *that was then, this is now.* Demonstrate current skills and valid reasons why you want the job.

How do I write a CV if I have just left full-time education with little real work experience?

Analyse every job or work-related activity including work placements, work shadowing, even workplace visits. Next, think hard about other life experiences and extra-curricular activity. Perhaps you organised complicated social events, competitions, or sporting activities, or you may have been a member of a society or club? Write about the skills you acquired from all these experiences. See also the suggested CV structure in Chapter 6, page 57.

How much should I say about my qualifications and learning history?

On the whole, employers see qualifications as a reflection of how well you can think and whether you take responsibility for your own learning and development. Often the words 'graduate' or 'professionally qualified' are enough to indicate you meet the standards required. If you have qualifications beyond A level you rarely need to list the subjects you studied at the age of 16 such as GCSEs. Don't mention qualifications or courses which have no conceivable connection to the job.

Often the question on a reader's mind is 'is this qualification useful?' A subject title on its own will rarely be an answer. A recruiter makes assumptions about the usefulness of your qualifications unless you specifically state what you achieved and learned (see also Chapter 12, page 127, for where this information best fits).

If you're applying for a role requiring a degree and you're not a graduate, ensure that the first page of your CV points to evidence that will convince a reader you have achieved the same standard, for example, work experience, training courses attended, on-the-job training.

Mention all relevant training, even if it wasn't certificated. Don't just list courses attended – say something interesting about them, and explain any courses that may be unclear. Be aware that just mentioning a training course is fairly weak skill evidence – whenever possible it's better to show how you've used the skills in work.

How should I mention a PhD?

Many employers express irritation at a non-medical CV that uses the term 'Dr'. Mention a PhD in your listed qualifications, and write about what makes it relevant, for example, the challenges you overcame, the expertise and niche knowledge it has provided.

What kind of personal information should I include?

In the UK market you will need to include very little personal information. Much of this information is material that employers aren't allowed to ask about anyway, and most of it is irrelevant. Do not provide details of your marital status and number or ages of children. For some roles it helps to confirm you have a full driving licence.

You don't need to include a full postal address as long as you provide your email details. Career coach Ruth Winden writes: 'In a world where identity fraud is a common threat, think carefully which details you share about yourself on your CV, especially if you post it online. Your address and contact details, plus your exact birthday date is all that criminals need to create severe havoc in your life.'

Should I mention my interests?

Some people include all kinds of quirky personal information including information about hobbies, pets, travel plans, being an advanced driver, religious affiliation, unfinished novels, prejudices, and obsessions. Is any of this relevant to a busy recruiter?

Kate Howlett writes: 'Keep interests relevant. There's a 50% chance that a reader is interested, so consider cutting them out if that helps you keep to two pages.' Mention interests that (a) are relevant to the job or (b) demonstrate social interaction or teamwork, or (c) point to a rounded life outside work.

Don't list any interests that you are not prepared to talk about with enthusiasm. Resist the bland lists seen by HR departments; one employer complained of 'interests such as reading and travel – we all read and travel!'. In contrast, another HR manager echoed a worry shared by many employers about candidates with no life outside work – sometimes this additional evidence creates a more authentic picture.

Should I identify referees on my CV?

This is not a good idea. Your CV may be copied, forwarded by email and generally passed along without your knowledge. You may not know when your referees are being approached. Keep control of this process: when references are going to be obtained, brief your referees on the job and remind them how you fit (sending your referee an up-to-date copy of your CV may help jog memory). Don't waste a line writing 'References available on request'. If an employer asks for referees, name them in a cover letter.

Should I mention health problems?

You are not required to provide information about your state of health on a CV. If you are asked direct questions about your health history at interview or in an application form, you must answer them honestly and accurately. Employers will typically ask about health conditions if you are being offered medical or health insurance, or being considered for a company pension scheme. You may, for example, be asked how many days of sick leave you had in the past two years. Take specialist advice if you need to declare a disability.

I can't get my CV to match the role. What do I do?

Often what's required here is a more thorough analysis of the job or better mining for evidence. If you've done both well and still can't get a match, the role may not be for you. If you put a false slant on your CV information, your evidence will come apart at interview. Remember that employers often over-specify jobs, asking for unrealistic levels of experience or suggesting that candidates need to cover every requirement – in reality they often only get a 75% fit, so it may be worth applying if you feel you cover most areas fairly well.

Final draft – checklists

Try writing a long version of your CV, and then cut it back. Don't rush the job. It takes a good four hours or so to put together a good, polished CV, and you can't do that in a single four-hour block. Draft, redraft, get feedback, draft again, check for a market reaction, finalise.

Eight top tips on bullet points

1 Communicate in the simplest language you can. Short words work best.
2 Vary the length of bullet points, mixing long and short to create variety and white space.
3 Put your strongest bullet point at the top or bottom of a list.
4 Put the strongest statement at the beginning of each paragraph or bullet point.
5 Avoid repeating words in the same bullet point.
6 Link your skill or achievement to a particular job or organisation to give it context.
7 Include tangible measures of achievement (profitability, turnover, time or money saved, customer satisfaction ratings, numbers, percentages, etc.).
8 Tighten up your language to convey the maximum information in the shortest space without your docu-

ment becoming uncomfortably abbreviated. Think 'email concise' rather than 'text speak'.

Style edit

■ Mention the names of well-known organisations if you've worked for or with them.
■ Don't list the same skill repeatedly over several jobs – vary your phrasing and maximise detail in the most recent job.
■ Don't list routine skills that are held by staff several rungs below you – reflect your seniority.
■ Make sure that your CV includes relevant keywords or phrases that might be hunted if your CV is being scanned electronically. (See Chapter 2, page 14, on white text for search engine optimisation.)
■ Don't repeat information in your CV. If you've said it, you've said it.
■ Avoid the word 'I' – it can sound like either a begging letter or an ego trip. (See Chapter 8, page 84, on the **smart third person**.)
■ Avoid obscure abbreviations, acronyms, or jargon.
■ Don't put yourself down, and don't try irony or humour. It rarely reads the way you want it to.
■ Don't apologise for any part of your CV. Don't demonstrate frustration, anger, or bitterness.
■ Don't include anything that strikes a negative note, particularly on page 1.

Presentation reminders

■ Don't write 'Curriculum Vitae' at the top.
■ Don't right-justify your CV (aligned text on the right-hand margin) – it makes it difficult to read quickly.
■ Use section headings if they help, but not to introduce elements which are obvious (for example, your profile).

- Check you have sufficient white space. Edit rather than trying to squeeze too much into one page.
- If you need a hard copy, print your CV on 100 gsm white paper – nothing fancier. Don't use poor quality photocopies.
- Make sure that paragraphs and bullet points are aligned and look neat.
- Don't bind your CV in a folder, laminate it or do anything with it other than staple the pages together in the top left-hand corner.

Final edit checklist

- Triple check your email address and phone number – if an employer can't find you the first time they may not try again.
- Check for inconsistencies in your work history. Do start and end dates match up?
- Are there any gaps between dates? Offer short, uncomplicated explanations for any gaps in your CV.
- Double check spellings, particularly the names of organisations and products.
- Use language which connects strongly to the job on offer.
- Ensure your CV looks good, is easy to read, and says what you want it to say in the first 15 words.

14 Market testing your CV and working with recruitment consultancies

This chapter helps you to:

- Road test your CV before you circulate it widely
- Anticipate interview questions arising from your CV
- Understand how recruitment consultancies will view your CV
- Know how to ask for the most useful CV feedback

> *'Advice is what we ask for when we already know the answer but we wish we didn't.'* Erica Jong

Market testing before wide circulation

Every day employers see CVs that are not market ready. At a basic level they may contain errors and gaps. These problems are relatively easily solved. Bigger issues arise when your CV doesn't do what you want it to do, perhaps because it tries to say too much, gives conflicting messages, says the wrong things, or says the right things in the wrong order.

No one would produce a corporate brochure or website without checking customer responses. You only need a small test group to give you insights into the reactions of users. Do the same for your CV. Before you send out dozens of copies, market test it.

Do this at the right point. You may still be finessing the profile, but the CV should be pretty finished, and pretty good. There's no point market testing a CV full of errors or gaps – people will miss the big problems by pointing out the small ones. When you feel the CV is as good as it can get, market test it by showing it to four or five people. Choose constructive and friendly people – not decision-makers in your network who might be put off by your first draft. Ideally, pick people who regularly read CVs (HR staff, line managers – and especially recruitment consultants). When you hand over your CV, *don't* explain it or outline what you hope it will achieve. Ask for blunt feedback about what the document communicates. This is the best way of predicting the response you'll get from a busy employer.

When you have received constructive feedback (see below for more on the difference between opinion and interpretation), your CV is probably about 95% there – which means you can begin to use it for job applications or speculative approaches. You can fine-tune the remaining 5% during your job search.

Interview problems arising from your CV

Too many candidates assume that an interview will connect in some way with their CVs. Some interviewers will make very little reference to it (and may not have read it in any depth), while others will go through it line by line.

Career coach Zena Everett draws on her recruitment experience when she writes: 'Make sure you know (inside out) the CV version the interviewer will be using. Ask a family member or friend to check that version and ask really obvious questions arising from it – so obvious you might not have spotted them yourself.'

If you're trying to anticipate what interview questions your CV will prompt, think in terms of positive and negative elements. Where you have presented positive facts that strongly match the job, an average interviewer may simply get you to talk them through. When retelling these stories, avoid using the words on paper – it's very dull to hear a candidate repeat CV phrases. Tell the stories in different language, and have some new material up your sleeve which you haven't used. Be aware that positive information may also prompt probing questions: what exactly did you do? What were you, personally, responsible for? Failure to anticipate probing questions is one of the factors that results in a weak CV – it lets you down when you need it most, in the interview room.

Negative information in a CV is a bigger problem. This might be the wrong information, or might be the lack of it. It may rule you out, or may lead to some very uncomfortable questions. So check your CV carefully, not just for the things that will rule you in, but also the things that rule you out. If there is something important missing, don't leave it out and hope for the best. Put in some compensating evidence, perhaps in a covering letter (for example, if you lack a specified qualification). Ask yourself 'what page 1 material might keep me off a shortlist?'. If you've secured an interview, ask yourself 'what things in my CV might this employer still be worried about?'.

For a comprehensive overview of interview preparation see my book *Job Interviews: Top Answers To Tough Questions*.

Working with recruitment consultancies

You will see frequent reference in this book to recruitment consultants. Recruitment consultancies vary widely, depending on the level of staff they place. At the lower end of the market you can find employment or staffing agencies mainly dealing with temporary work. Recruitment consultancies tend to work in the mid-range, while those at the executive end are called selection or search consultancies (or 'headhunters'). All these organisations are paid by employers to find staff (in the UK these organisations are not allowed to charge a fee to job seekers).

Recruitment consultants can help your job search considerably, sometimes by placing you straight on to a shortlist. Knowing two things about them will help your approach. First, they are almost always vacancy-driven – they have jobs to fill, and this is their primary focus. Second, recruitment consultants are at heart sales people, therefore you will make progress with them when they have got to know you a little and feel that they can 'sell' you to an employer. This means that you need to take every opportunity to have a conversation, by phone and in person. Listen to market advice – but cross-check it against what you hear from others.

Everything you do with a recruitment consultancy should be about building relationships; agencies say that shortlists often include one candidate who isn't an exact match to the job but that person has great transferable skills and makes a big impression at interview. You don't move forward much by just emailing a CV. Some candidates do this and then get very tetchy if they don't receive an instant response connecting them to suitable vacancies. Consultants don't always pool candidate information, and a CV won't automatically be cross-referenced against every job on the books. Equally, don't be overwhelmed by a positive response. Recruiters are upbeat and naturally encourage or even flatter candidates. Some over-promise and then under-deliver. Don't be put off by this – an indifferent agency can still land you a brilliant job.

Asking agencies for feedback on your CV

Showing your CV to a recruitment consultant is a great form of market testing. If several experienced consultants give you the same advice, that's data. However, a lot of what you'll hear is widely varying opinions on CV style and layout. Don't get distracted; if you try to accommodate all views you'll end up rewriting your CV after every interview.

Don't ask for an opinion on your CV – ask for a summary. Ask a recruitment consultant 'What does my CV say to you?'. Listen carefully to the story coming back at you. If it makes sense, your CV is working. If the consultant says 'I'm not sure' or 'it's pulling in several different directions', you've got work to do.

How recruitment consultants react to page 1

Some recruitment consultants dislike any kind of profile on a CV. Jeff Grout, experienced recruiter, business consultant, and author of *Recruiting Excellence* argues that a profile is 'purely subjective – the candidate is not going to say anything negative about themselves – and disregarded by most recruiters'. Another recruitment specialist states: 'Please, no personal introduction describing in a surfeit of adjectives how wonderful you are. An experienced recruiter never reads it; they are the ones who are expected to assess your ability, not you.'

Joëlle Warren, Executive Chairman of Warren Partners Executive Search, writes: 'I don't like profiles that are full of superlatives, but I have come to like summaries that give a view of what the person is looking for, "Marketing Director with strong commercial background in FMCG and retail sector seeking General Management role which plays to international experience within a blue chip environment" for example is OK but then ones that say "Highly motivated and inspirational leader with outstanding communication skills etc." are still not my cup of tea. We're inundated with CVs from job seekers and it's even more important to make clear who you are and what you're looking for "at a glance". Don't assume your covering letter will be read – ensure the CV stands alone. Make sure it's really easy to get hold of you – you'd be amazed how many people don't have their contact details at the top but hidden away in a header or footer. I've also discovered that those people who can't condense their CVs into two sides (maximum three) also find it difficult to give concise answers to questions at interview!'

Joëlle Warren also adds: 'As far as a list of achievements is concerned I prefer seeing them against each role but what I do encourage on page 1 is giving a flavour of the whole career. So, for example, if they are an MD but from a financial background and the financial roles are further back on the CV, or if they are currently at an SME but have a background in blue chips, I would recommend they include a career summary encapsulated on page 1 so vital information doesn't need to be dug around for.'

Recruitment specialist Linda Clark of The Human Choice writes: 'Employers can afford to be very choosy in the current market so a good-looking and well-structured CV – of course with relevant experience – is crucial. When good candidates are out of work or doing consultancy or interim roles, and so not on the immediate radar screen of a headhunter, a CV must stand out. I recommend candidates are tighter with their focus and the need to "sell" themselves upfront in a good profile is more essential than ever.'

Speculative letters to recruitment consultants

A speculative letter is often a good way of getting your job-search story across to a busy recruitment consultant. Instead of referring to a specific organisation or role, use a more general heading, for example, 'Management roles in the health/fitness sector'. As with other speculative letters (see Chapter 15, page 164) you're dealing with a busy reader, so focus on a handful of strong points.

Spot agencies who regularly advertise jobs in your chosen sector. Find the individual consultants who are handling specific roles. Administrators will discourage you from speaking to them, but you will often get through if you need to ask a detailed or technical question about the role advertised. State *very briefly* what you are looking for, and what you have to offer. Afterwards, email your CV with a strong cover letter and phone up again in a couple of days' time to ensure the CV has been received, and ideally to build on the relationship.

Example speculative letter to a recruitment consultant

An example speculative letter is shown opposite.

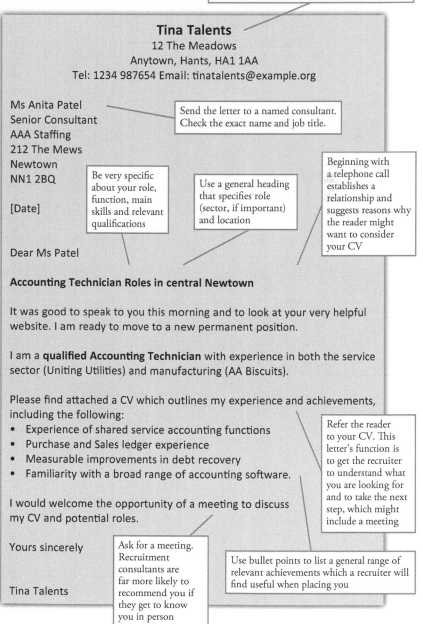

Full, clear contact details – including a postal address if you send it by post. An email cover letter to an agency can use your standard email sign off, which should include the same top line contact information as your CV.

Tina Talents
12 The Meadows
Anytown, Hants, HA1 1AA
Tel: 1234 987654 Email: tinatalents@example.org

Ms Anita Patel
Senior Consultant
AAA Staffing
212 The Mews
Newtown
NN1 2BQ

[Date]

Dear Ms Patel

Send the letter to a named consultant. Check the exact name and job title.

Be very specific about your role, function, main skills and relevant qualifications

Use a general heading that specifies role (sector, if important) and location

Beginning with a telephone call establishes a relationship and suggests reasons why the reader might want to consider your CV

Accounting Technician Roles in central Newtown

It was good to speak to you this morning and to look at your very helpful website. I am ready to move to a new permanent position.

I am a **qualified Accounting Technician** with experience in both the service sector (Uniting Utilities) and manufacturing (AA Biscuits).

Please find attached a CV which outlines my experience and achievements, including the following:

- Experience of shared service accounting functions
- Purchase and Sales ledger experience
- Measurable improvements in debt recovery
- Familiarity with a broad range of accounting software.

I would welcome the opportunity of a meeting to discuss my CV and potential roles.

Yours sincerely

Tina Talents

Refer the reader to your CV. This letter's function is to get the recruiter to understand what you are looking for and to take the next step, which might include a meeting

Ask for a meeting. Recruitment consultants are far more likely to recommend you if they get to know you in person

Use bullet points to list a general range of relevant achievements which a recruiter will find useful when placing you

Key points from this chapter

✓ Road test your CV, but don't get distracted by conflicting opinions on CV structure.

✓ Understand what agencies can – and cannot – do for you.

✓ The format of your CV is far less important than the relationship you build with a recruitment consultant.

✓ Prepare a straight-in CV in case an agency demands it.

✓ Otherwise keep shaping your profile so that it works for recruitment consultants as well as a more general audience.

15

Speculative and cover letters

This chapter helps you to:

- Understand the structure of a good cover letter
- Avoid classic errors in letters that get you rejected at the first hurdle
- Write a brief, focused cover letter that presents your CV in the best light
- Explore the value of speculative approaches

'The two words "information" and "communication" are often used interchangeably, but they signify quite different things. Information is giving out; communication is getting through.' Sydney J. Harris

Why your CV needs help

No matter how brilliant your CV, it still needs an introduction. If it's in response to an advertisement, you will need a cover letter to connect your personal information with the specific vacancy.

The first mistake made when writing cover letters is to believe that the letter will sell you into the job. It won't. If you're lucky, it will simply persuade the reader to consider your CV. If it's a good letter, it will flag up three or four strong items in your CV worth considering.

The second mistake is to believe that you should rehearse every reason you're suitable for the job. Some candidates send in cover letters over two pages long, crammed with information. Don't make the mistake of thinking that the longer you argue your case, the better your chances of an interview. The opposite is almost certainly the case. If you can't write a one-page letter convincing someone to read your CV, how effective will your communication skills be in the job?

Classic problems with cover letters

Despite all the advice available, people keep making the same mistakes when sending cover letters:

- Standard wording which makes little connection to the job.
- Too long, packed with superfluous information.
- Working too hard and too obviously to sell themselves into an interview.

Reminders when you send a cover letter with your CV

Your letter *should say more about the employer than it says about you*. State why you are attracted to an employer. Use your letter as an opportunity to explain why your skills and experience might be useful, if this is not clear from your CV. Again, don't list every matching factor. Try to work out the top half dozen or so priorities in the employer's mind (see Chapter 2, pages 20–21 on analysing a job advertisement) and offer five or six matching pieces of evidence in your cover letter.

You may also want to address significant barriers at this point. For example, if you do not have the relevant qualifications required, you will probably want to use a letter to outline how your experience provides you with the skills and know-how necessary to do the job.

When it comes to submitting your CV online, recruiters will often complain that they receive a cover letter that is in a separate file and that this takes extra time and trouble to open. It may be simpler to make your email message itself into a cover letter. Even in the age of email, sometimes it's smart to also send a nicely printed CV and cover letter by post.

Cover letter tips

Things to avoid in cover letters

■ Don't use tired opening phrases like 'This letter is written in response to' or 'Please consider this application for the position of'.

■ Don't begin 'Dear sir/madam' or 'To whom it may concern'. Find the name of the person it should go to. If it's addressed to a named individual ('Dear Mr Smith') it needs to end with 'Yours sincerely'.

■ Don't repeat phrases from your CV – reword and summarise.

■ Don't apologise in your letter for the lack of a qualification or for your age, and don't refer to negative aspects such as why you left your last job.

■ Don't be hesitant – phrases like 'I think' and 'perhaps' communicate lack of clarity.

■ Don't be over-assertive (for example, 'I will expect a call').

■ Don't beg for an interview or offer special pleading (for example, 'please read this application carefully').

Things to include in cover letters

■ Quote the exact job title and reference, and make sure your letter is addressed to the right person. Double check the spelling of the recipient's name.

- Emphasise key pieces of information using bold text or bullet points, but not excessively.
- Proof-read your cover letter for accuracy as diligently as you read your CV.
- Keep your letter brief and to the point, another way of answering the question: why you? (The 'so what?' test from Chapter 12, page 131, works well here.)

The structure of a good cover letter

A well-structured letter is shown opposite.

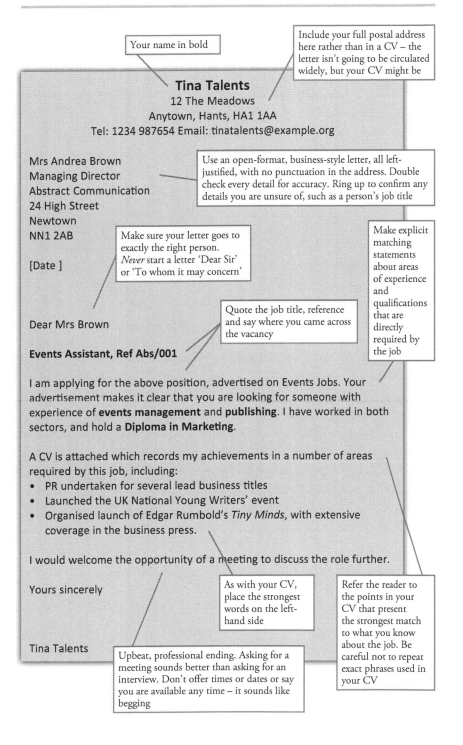

Your name in bold

Include your full postal address here rather than in a CV – the letter isn't going to be circulated widely, but your CV might be

Tina Talents
12 The Meadows
Anytown, Hants, HA1 1AA
Tel: 1234 987654 Email: tinatalents@example.org

Mrs Andrea Brown
Managing Director
Abstract Communication
24 High Street
Newtown
NN1 2AB

Use an open-format, business-style letter, all left-justified, with no punctuation in the address. Double check every detail for accuracy. Ring up to confirm any details you are unsure of, such as a person's job title

[Date]

Make sure your letter goes to exactly the right person. *Never* start a letter 'Dear Sir' or 'To whom it may concern'

Make explicit matching statements about areas of experience and qualifications that are directly required by the job

Dear Mrs Brown

Quote the job title, reference and say where you came across the vacancy

Events Assistant, Ref Abs/001

I am applying for the above position, advertised on Events Jobs. Your advertisement makes it clear that you are looking for someone with experience of **events management** and **publishing**. I have worked in both sectors, and hold a **Diploma in Marketing**.

A CV is attached which records my achievements in a number of areas required by this job, including:
- PR undertaken for several lead business titles
- Launched the UK National Young Writers' event
- Organised launch of Edgar Rumbold's *Tiny Minds*, with extensive coverage in the business press.

I would welcome the opportunity of a meeting to discuss the role further.

Yours sincerely

As with your CV, place the strongest words on the left-hand side

Refer the reader to the points in your CV that present the strongest match to what you know about the job. Be careful not to repeat exact phrases used in your CV

Tina Talents

Upbeat, professional ending. Asking for a meeting sounds better than asking for an interview. Don't offer times or dates or say you are available any time – it sounds like begging

Speculative letters

A speculative letter is one way of communicating with an employer who is not currently advertising for staff. The wrong kind of speculative letter is a waste of paper – a poorly targeted message gives you poor results, if any. Most untargeted letters or emails have made little or no attempt to understand the needs of the organisation, and are instantly considered as junk mail.

Speculative letters (by post or email) can work better than you might think. You should, however, consider whether a letter is the best route available to you. If you can get close to a decision-maker through personal contacts, networking will always be more effective than writing. Letters and CVs always work best as a back-up to a conversation, ideally one conducted face to face.

However, there are times when the quickest and simplest way of getting your details in front of a decision-maker is to send in a carefully targeted letter. As with cover letters in general, the focus should be on matching a shortlist of what the employer needs against what you have to offer. Start by saying what drew the organisation to your attention – find something positive that is recent news. Then, briefly, draw the employer's attention to the top half dozen or so facts about you that are most likely to trigger the response 'let's get this candidate in'. A small burst of evidence works because a busy decision-maker is unlikely to read any further.

When a speculative letter might work

There are three times when speculative letters are effective:

1 When you have skills and experience which are in short supply. Employers will often create positions for skilled people just to get them into the organisation.

2 Where your research has flagged up target organisations which appear to be a strong match to your skill set.

3 Where you already have networked your way to a contact at an organisation and you are writing to confirm or add to what they already know about you.

Speculative letters have a double effect. They may get you a meeting with an employer but, even if they don't, they improve your visibility in the hidden job market. You're planting important information in the memory of people capable of making recommendations. Even if they only lead to a conversation where you ask 'who else should I be talking to?', the letter has worked.

How to find target organisations for your speculative letters

Approaches to organisations who are not advertising should be part of your multi-strategy job-search (see Chapter 2, page 12). Finding organisations is part of that activity. The least productive way of finding them is from directories or websites. You get better results asking current and former work colleagues and everyone else you encounter in your job search. Keep asking about sectors, sub-sectors, linked and partner organisations. In addition, look around you – drive round your local area and take note of organisations. Read your regional or specialist press, taking note of any organisations named. Keep researching and digging, and always with one end in mind: the name and job title of a decision-maker, and enough information about the organisation for you to make a credible application.

When a speculative letter probably won't work

If you are unclear about why you are applying, unsure about what there is in your experience that might interest a recruiter or if you just don't know enough about an organisation to write a convincing letter, then don't waste everyone's time.

Similarly, you may discover that the organisation has a policy of ignoring all speculative letters because every application needs to be formally processed. Some organisations will only consider application forms, and only when specific posts are advertised. In this case you are best (a) applying for specific positions following the organisation's rules or (b) networking your way to a face-to-face conversation.

Problems with most speculative letters

As the reader of a speculative letter has no real motive for reading your letter, it matters that you get it right. Too many employers receive the wrong kind of letters:

- Entirely focused on the writer.
- Standard letters that do not relate to a specific job or employer.
- Sent to the wrong person.
- With a CV mentioning a target job not relevant to this employer.
- Containing an unfocused message.
- Failing to give a value reason for reading the CV.
- Over-selling.

A suggested format is set out below. Note that this follows most of the basics of the outline cover letter discussed earlier.

The structure of a good speculative letter to an employer

A good speculative letter is shown opposite.

Full contact details again

Tina Talents
12 The Meadows
Anytown, Hants, HA1 1AA
Tel: 1234 987654 Email: tinatalents@example.org

Mr Andrew Smith
Technical Director
ABC Components Ltd
Main Drive
Newtown
NN1 2CD

Your letter must go direct to the top decision-maker, not the HR department. Check the exact name and job title of the person you want to write to

[Date]

Focus on something the reader should be proud of. A good letter also focuses on the employer, not you. Avoid beginning every paragraph with 'I'

Focus on the *needs* of the employer. Make it crystal clear what kind of role you want to fill, and throw in a summary of your relevant experience

Dear Mr Smith

It was impressive to note in the industry press that ABC Components has won the ZZA contract.

At times like this effective controls on **purchasing** can make a huge difference. I am a **Senior Purchasing Professional** with experience in both pharmaceuticals and electronics.

Please find attached a CV which outlines my experience and achievements in a number of areas, including:
- Implementing a new e-purchasing function
- Achieving £12K savings over 36 months on a total spend of £200K
- Recruiting and motivating a team of purchasing professionals.

I would welcome the opportunity of a meeting to discuss how I can contribute to your organisation.

Yours sincerely

Tina Talents

Upbeat ending which asks for a meeting

Use bullet points to list a range of attractive and relevant achievements to persuade the reader to look at your CV

Refer the reader to your CV. The only function of this letter is to get your CV read, and to get you an interview with a decision-maker

(See also Chapter 14, page 157 for an example of a speculative letter to a recruitment consultant.)

Gain a new perspective on speculative and cover letters

Before you send your letter, read it from the perspective of a busy employer. You may have spent hours crafting it, but your letter will be skim-read – in seconds. Is it clear why you are writing, and what you hope to achieve? Can it be said in fewer words? Are you trying to make too many points?

■ *Don't make the letter entirely about you.* Too many covering and speculative letters are written entirely from the applicant's point of view – every paragraph begins with the word 'I'. Instead, say what about the organisation has attracted you. Employers spend a great deal of money trying to get noticed, so telling them that their budget was well spent is not a bad move.

■ Give a *value reason* for writing – a good reason why someone should read your speculative letter. If you're writing a speculative letter where there is no advertised vacancy, say what attracted you in the first place, otherwise it sounds like your only motivation is wanting a job. If you're writing a speculative letter to a recruitment consultant, say how you have come across them (sometimes it helps to mention an organisation or senior manager who recommended this particular agency).

Key points from this chapter

✓ Most cover letters are too long, too pushy, or too desperate.

✓ A good cover letter gives four or five strong reasons why an organisation should see you.

✓ Speculative letters (or emails) can be door openers if they are well researched and well pitched.

✓ Make sure the focus of the letter is 'you' and not 'I'.

16

Completing application forms

This chapter helps you to:

- Communicate your strengths within the constraints of an application form
- Draw on your CV data bank to complete application forms
- Manage requests for competency information
- Complete the 'supporting statement' section so you'll get shortlisted

'Words are, of course, the most powerful drug used by mankind.' Rudyard Kipling

Know the form

If you're job seeking you'll spend a lot of time filling in complicated application forms, often online. They are frustrating and consume a great deal of time, sometimes with no feedback at all. However, if you need to complete an application form to have any chance of getting shortlisted, there's no way round the process. What many candidates don't realise is that there is an art to completing these forms in such a way that you tick the right boxes on the selector's shortlist.

Start by reading through the whole form quickly so you know what information you will need at your fingertips. It's frustrating to get halfway through an online form to realise that you don't have some vital detail.

Don't reinvent the wheel

When completing the form you will, of course, need the same facts that populate your CV: dates and grades of qualifications, names of employers, job titles, and dates of employment. Read the instructions very carefully. For example, the form may require you to give the exact dates of your employment history, or grades of qualifications you took at the age of 16. You might also be required to include other information not in your CV, for example the full postal address of past employers.

However, most of the information you will need to include will be job information which you should already have on file. If you have completed the **CV data bank** in Chapter 4, page 37, you will have a wealth of material available to you to assist when completing an application form, allowing you to cut and paste basic information such as your job history.

As with any process where you're matching yourself against an employer's needs, don't get bogged down in the detail. When you submit a CV you are generally aiming to match yourself against between six and eight requirements, and the same thing is true when you are completing an application form. Read job requirements carefully so you can see the wood from the trees – sort out the small number of things that appear to be essential items on the employer's shopping list.

When including information, ensure that you include everything requested. If you fail to provide something that has been asked for, including relatively trivial information, your form might be excluded. For example, if asked to list the date and grade achieved for every qualification you hold, do so.

Application form layout

When recording job information, layout permitting, use bullet points to capture particular achievements – just as you would in a CV. However, sometimes with online documents it's impossible to use text effects such as bullet points. In this case you might lay text out using asterisks to start each section, use separate lines, or even number key points in the text itself, for example: *'Responsible for (1) staff development and appraisal, (2) induction training of all new recruits and (3) development of new staff starter pack.'*

Remember that the completed form will be read at high speed. Emphasise key information. If you are invited to submit a covering letter, use that to show how you match the employer's top six requirements – see Chapter 15, page 159.

Checking and submitting the form

Complete the form promptly, and make sure it is returned by the deadline. Print off or photocopy the completed form so you can have a copy with you if you are called to interview.

Making your story come to life in an application form
- Save online forms regularly in case the system crashes or your Internet connection drops.
- Use the same strategies you have used in CV writing to turn your experience into evidence which is not only relevant but interesting.
- Feel free to use the first person – 'I'. The punchy CV third person does not fit an application form which clearly asks you to state *your* experience and *your* fit for the job.
- Don't assume that people understand your past jobs – job titles give very little away. Use bullet points to draw out the impact you made.

- Ensure you match evidence throughout the form against the job.
- Use bullet points where appropriate rather than long paragraphs of text.
- Match the language and terminology you use to the job. Sometimes it pays to repeat key words and phrases used in the job documentation.
- Concentrate on composing the supporting statement, or whatever part of the form allows you to explain in detail why you match the role.
- After cutting and pasting, proof-read carefully to ensure that the material is complete, correct, and relates to this job not a previous one you applied for.

The main statement

The critical part of any application form may be a section titled 'Other information', 'Supporting statement', or simply a large box on the form inviting you to explain why your experience matches the job. Sometimes you will be asked to match yourself against a prescribed list of competencies; at other times you are simply given a blank space to explain to a selector why you fit the main requirements of the role.

This part of the form, whether it is at the front or the back, is your primary opportunity to 'pitch' your strengths. This section has the same important function as the first half page of your CV, but in this case you are matching yourself against *one particular job*. Generalised statements or a cut and paste from your CV won't do.

Examine job documentation carefully, including the job advertisement. Use a highlighter pen to spot words which provide big clues about what the employer considers vital. Below are four strategies for completing the 'Supporting statement' depending on the way the job description and person specification are structured:

Completing the 'supporting statement' section of an application form

1 **Where there is a list of up to 10 competencies.** Use each competency (or defined skill, knowledge area, or personal quality) as a sub-heading, using the exact terms of the job description. Against each sub-heading give one or two concrete examples of where you have demonstrated what's required, for example:

Effective Written Communication
My recent role required me to produce formal reports for a range of audiences including our Trustees and members. I wrote the Membership Services section of our 2012 Annual Report and several pages of our current website. I have written articles on conservation for the regional and national press.

2 **Where there is a list of more than 10 competencies.** The problem here is that some jobs list 20 or more competencies. If you are asked to match each of them, point by point, then do so. Failure to follow this direction could mean that your application form is excluded, early, probably by a junior member of staff who has been given a checklist for how to exclude forms. If you are not given precise information about how much information to give, you will probably assume that writing extensive evidence against 20 or 30 competencies is going to result in far too much material. This is an important judgement call, and you might consider ringing the employer to ask for advice about what, exactly, they want. Some candidates take a strategy of grouping competencies together, for example:

Leadership, People, and Change Management
In my role as Department Head I have been required to lead a creative team through a time of considerable change for the organisation. My approach has been to consult widely, both one-to-one and in team discussions, and to encourage groups to come forward with solutions as well as problems. I also introduced a programme of twice-monthly staff briefings to ensure clear and rapid communication through the reorganisation. I was called on to demonstrate leadership qualities when I was required to implement staffing and resource cutbacks, and worked hard to ensure that difficult news was communicated in a timely and sensitive manner.

Another approach is to give detailed evidence in relation to what you consider to be the most important skills, and summary information (using bullet points if possible) in relation to background requirements, for example:

Systems, Data, and Information Management

This role requires a range of competencies relating to use of systems, information management and retrieval. My experience includes the following achievements:

- Organised a database of 7,000 members as Membership Team Leader for the IOTP.
- Supervised the handling of member enquiries.
- Membership team praised in the ITP annual report for generating the largest number of innovations in 2011.
- Organised a migration of data to a new software platform.
- Managed the transfer of 7,500 member records within 6 weeks, cross-checked for accuracy, with a measured 44% improvement in member satisfaction ratings.

3 **Where there is no defined list of competencies but some information about skills and qualities.** Interrogate documents carefully until you identify what you consider to be the most important 6–10 requirements, and use these as sub-headings as in (1) above.

4 **Where there is vague information about skills and qualities.** Even if skills or competencies are not formally listed, you can usually draw out big clues from job advertisements. For example, if the job ad states 'the post holder will need a track record of B2B business development' you know that you will need to demonstrate the ability to identify and win new business-to-business customers, win deals, and build long-term sales relationships. Those are your starter headings.

Key points from this chapter

✓ Use your **CV data bank** as a master file for both your CV and application forms.

✓ Pay particular attention to high-emphasis employer requirements.

✓ Communicate your strong match to the job, and a clear reason why it's a natural next step for you.

✓ Write a well-structured response to the 'supporting statement' section, if necessary drawing on evidence of competencies.

Employer responses to the CV survey

This chapter helps you to:

- Understand how employers interpret CVs
- Spot employer likes and dislikes
- Understand what might result in your CV being excluded quickly
- Hear employer views on tricky CV issues

> *'All my life I've looked at words as though I were seeing them for the first time.'*   Ernest Hemingway

Research on what employers want to see in a CV

How do you decide what your CV should contain? Ask an employer.

This book draws on specially commissioned research conducted with the kind assistance of Career Management Consultants Ltd (CMC), one of the UK's top outplacement companies and now part of the Savile Group. CMC's specialism is outplacement (career coaching for executives and senior managers, paid for by the organisations who are making them redundant). CMC asked 7300 senior HR staff and line managers for their views.

What employers find immediately off-putting

Here are some of the things employers say will guarantee that your CV will be rejected immediately:

- Lack of tailoring. 'The electronic age means that often no real thought goes into submitting an application – you can just bang it out to a number of companies via email.'
- 'People just sending in a CV with no covering letter indicating which post they are applying for.'
- 'CVs that look as if they came out of a book, for example, *'I'm a team player but I can work alone'*.
- 'Profiles that are just standard wording.'
- 'Too much irrelevant personal information, for example, names of children.'
- 'CVs with acronyms, particularly technical terms, where initials can have several meanings.'
- 'Copies of certificates, including Scouts knot badge.'
- 'Dump of detailed job descriptions for every job held.'
- 'CVs put together years ago and updated in pen.'
- 'Gimmicks (for example, attaching a teabag and a message which says "have a cup of tea while you read this"). I even heard of someone sending half a £50 note saying the other half would be handed over at interview!'
- 'CVs on coloured paper, using lots of different fonts … People think it makes them come across as a fun person but I feel it shows a lack of professionalism.'
- 'Cutting and pasting from other applications without changing the company's name!'
- 'Over-egging skills and achievements … Over-the-top selling of candidates' abilities in CV jargon.'
- 'People applying for a role when they are not available for six months to a year.'
- 'Language used that is more suitable to a dating agency!'

By post or by email?

About half of employers want to see your CV arrive by email, but a third either have no preference or are happy to receive a CV by post.

Be as careful with an email covering letter as you would be with one sent on paper. Note, however, the views of one respondent: 'Email is great but does allow people to be more sloppy when submitting information. Candidates often submit their CVs for vacancies regardless of whether or not they really want the job. No care is taken and the CVs often bear no relation to the job on offer.'

Ninety-three per cent of employers want to see an email address listed on a CV.

Who will read my CV?

In answer to the question 'Who performs the first sift of CVs in your organisation?' the survey revealed that only just over half of CVs sent to organisations are read by HR staff (55%), and 29% are read by line managers.

The message seems to be that if you know your CV is more likely to be read by a line manager, write it with that person in mind. However, in most cases it needs to appeal both to an HR specialist *and* a line manager – therefore expressing both experience and competencies.

How many pages?

Two-thirds of employers would prefer your CV to be **no more than two pages long**. Only 20% feel that a CV of three pages is acceptable, 8% have no preference. Only 3% of HR specialists would like to see a CV expressed in just one page. One respondent indicated that he had received a 45-page CV.

Presentation

Over 90% of employers dislike receiving a photograph with your CV. A photograph creates legal problems for employers as it immediately communicates gender, race, and age.

Your CV needs to be business standard: clear, well laid out, easy to read, and avoiding errors which suggest poor attention to detail. One HR manager proved that there is an exception to every rule: 'I was most impressed by a candidate who at the time clearly did not have access to a PC and submitted a beautifully handwritten detailed CV. He had clearly taken the time and effort to do this for each position he was applying for – the CV submitted was an original, not copied, and tailored to the requirements of the job. Needless to say, he got an interview on the strength of this.'

Ninety-nine per cent of employers do *not* welcome a CV in a binder or cover because it needs to be removed before photocopying.

Creative approaches

A CV that tries to be visually innovative may stand out for all the wrong reasons. It draws attention to its quirkiness, not the information it contains. Special effects including tables, boxes or columns, graphics or cartoons are inadvisable, and will lead to problems if your CV is read by a computer. The exception is if you work in a visually creative field – in which case your skills should be evident on your website, Facebook page and, if you need one, your CV.

Summary information on page 1

Some employers say they dislike profiles on the first page of CVs. One wrote that 'personal summaries are irritating – they take up valuable space and no one is ever going to say they are not a team player or enthusiastic or capable! I never give them any credence.' Another view was that 'profiles at the start of many CVs read like the foreword of a Superman novel'. Another complained that profiles were often just a repeat of historical information contained elsewhere in the CV.

However, more than 80% of HR specialists like to see a short profile or summary on the first page of the CV. Seventy-seven per cent say they like to see primary achievements listed on the first page, and only 7% said they did not find this information useful.

What order should I list my jobs in?

Most employers (73%) prefer to see your most recent job listed first.

Things you do outside work

It's worth listing details of voluntary activities. Ninety per cent of employers are either happy to see information of this kind or have no strong feelings either way. Eight-four per cent are prepared to look at details of your hobbies.

One respondent took a positive view: 'I want to know a bit about them as a person: travel, pastimes, as well as qualifications and experience.' Others complained about too much irrelevant personal information.

Listing your competencies

Employers often ask candidates information about competencies. Some CVs offer a list of half a dozen or so competencies on page 1 in order to provide this information immediately. Just over half of employers find this a useful addition to a CV.

A CV that has obviously been written by a professional CV writing service

A number of employers expressed frustration with professionally written CVs. One manager found them 'too polished'. Seventy-one per cent of employers disagreed with the suggestion that a professionally written CV is useful. Many employers clearly include in this bracket CVs written by recruitment or career companies. One respondent wrote 'Many CVs from people sharing the same professional CV advice will look the same and use identical "search-enhancing" words and phrases.'

Another employer stated: 'It is not unusual to receive a professionally produced, word-perfect CV, which has clearly not been produced by the candidate, accompanied by an email containing several very basic spelling errors.' If someone is preparing a CV on your behalf, check it and market test it before agreeing that it can be sent on. One HR manager wrote that 'employment agencies who edit CVs on behalf of candidates often alter the documents so they misrepresent applicants'. Many employers dislike agency-submitted CVs because they 'refer to the candidate as a number'.

References

Some CVs include the names and addresses of referees. The research indicated that this is preferred by less than a third of employers. Many would rather you didn't waste space including this information, so the clear view is that references shouldn't be included in a CV. As Chapter 13 suggested, if you put the names of referees on every CV you send out you will quickly lose control of the process because you won't know when referees are being approached. Give out the names of referees only when you are asked for them.

Qualifications

Many CVs begin with information about qualifications, particularly CVs written by school, college, and university leavers. Roughly a third of employers would prefer to see details of grades, a third are indifferent, and a third would rather not be sent this information. There is no suggestion that employers are any more interested in A level grades than in GCSE grades. One employer commented that 'many candidates are learning to put themselves "up front" rather than their academic history'.

Languages

If you have strong spoken languages relevant to the role, list them – 81% of employers are interested.

Willingness to relocate

A surprising 70% of employers actively want to know from a CV whether you are prepared to relocate for a new job.

Age-related information

Many candidates are confused about what age-related infor- mation the law allows employers to request. Some candidates believe that they should not include any dates in their CVs at all. The evidence suggests that this strategy will get your CV excluded by most employers. Only 46% of HR professionals want dates for jobs you did over 10 years ago, but most still require important dates, as follows:

■ Start and end dates for different roles: 97%.
■ Date a degree or professional qualification was obtained: 60%.

Telling the truth

Employers report that candidates provide untrue information about job titles, accountability within positions, dates, achievements, and even hobbies. Nearly half of employers believe that some candidates lie about qualifications.

Covering letters

'Poor quality or overly obsequious covering letters' were criticised by one HR team. Others complained of long and unfocused letters, many containing errors.

How does this survey help you?

Our CV survey provides a great starting point for writing a CV that achieves its purpose. It helps you know what will get your CV excluded, and reinforces the fact that strong CVs point to details which are entirely relevant to the job, supported with hard evidence of skills, achievement, and knowledge. Employers are positively influenced by well-structured CVs free of inaccuracies and irrelevant information. Most actively welcome summarised information on page 1.

Index